The God Frequency

Shree Shambav's Vision of the One

VOLUME I

From Particle to Presence. From Code to Consciousness.

SHREE SHAMBAV

The God Frequency
Shree Shambav's Vision of the One
Volume One

Shree Shambav

Published by Shree Shambav, Tamil Nadu, India
Shree Shambav Ink & Imagination "Where Words Breathe and Imagination Soars"

First Edition, 2026

ISBN: 978-93-5812-631-0
Email:shreeshambav@gmail.com
Web:www.shambav.org

DEDICATION

"Isavasyam idam sarvam yat kim ca jagatyam jagat, tena tyaktena bhunjitha, ma gridhah kasyasvid dhanam"

To the Almighty,

the Divine Masters,

the family who listens,

and my parents who see –

your presence shapes the pages of my life's journey.

"Isavasyam idam sarvam yat kim ca jagatyam jagat"

Meaning: "God encompasses everything you perceive, see, or touch with your sense organs."

DISCLAIMER

The God Frequency: Shree Shambav's Vision of the One is a philosophical, spiritual, and contemplative exploration of consciousness, unity, ethics, and human awakening. It arises from integrative reflection upon ancient wisdom traditions, modern inquiry, lived experience, and meditative insight. This work is offered as an invitation to contemplation, inner inquiry, and self-understanding, not as a declaration of absolute or final truth.

The content of this book is intended solely for philosophical reflection, spiritual exploration, and educational enrichment. While it engages with themes from science, psychology, ethics, ecology, artificial intelligence, and metaphysics, it does not present itself as scientific doctrine, empirical validation, or professional authority. Nothing contained herein should be interpreted as medical, psychological, legal, financial, technical, or therapeutic advice, nor as a substitute for consultation with qualified professionals.

Although every effort has been made to present ideas with clarity, integrity, and depth, the author makes no guarantees regarding the accuracy, completeness, or universal applicability of the interpretations offered. The insights and perspectives shared are contemplative and integrative in nature, encouraging readers to engage critically, reflect inwardly, and interpret independently. Any conclusions, beliefs, or personal applications drawn from this work remain solely the responsibility of the reader.

Discussions of consciousness, suffering, destiny, ethics, artificial intelligence, and spiritual awakening may invite deep reflection or challenge existing assumptions. Such responses are a natural part of philosophical and spiritual engagement and are intended to foster awareness, humility, and insight, not certainty, dogma, or psychological distress. Readers are encouraged to approach the material with openness, discernment, and contemplative responsibility.

This book does not seek to persuade, convert, or impose belief. It does not claim authority over scientific, philosophical, or spiritual truth. Rather, it offers a contemplative framework — a lens of perception — through which readers may explore the inner architecture of consciousness and the deeper coherence of existence.

Ultimately, *The God Frequency* is shared in a spirit of reverence and inquiry, trusting the reader's wisdom to integrate what resonates, question what does not, and engage with the text as a living dialogue rather than a fixed conclusion.

Note: For knowledge and contemplative purposes only.

Note - If any part of the book, in any sequence, hurts the reader's sentiments, it would be just out of a sheer accident not intentional

EPIGRAPH

Before belief, there is vibration.

Before doctrine, there is coherence.

Before the seeker, there is the listening itself.

The God Frequency reminds us that truth is not discovered through distance, but through alignment—and that what we call God has always been the silent rhythm by which we exist, think, love, and return.

– Shree Shambav

The God Frequency

Shree Shambav's Vision of the One

VOLUME I

From Particle to Presence. From Code to Consciousness.

SHREE SHAMBAV

Shree Shambav is a 132x best-selling author, renowned for his transformative works in personal development and spiritual growth

Dear Cherished Readers

Dear Cherished Readers,

As I embark on this new literary voyage, my heart swells with profound gratitude and an overwhelming sense of connection. With deep emotion, I extend my heartfelt appreciation to each of you who has joined me on this journey.

With sincere warmth, I invite you to revisit the steps we have taken together through the pages of my earlier works. Our odyssey began with "Journey of Soul - Karma," a book that marked my first foray into the world of words and a testament to the raw passion that ignited my writing adventure.

The subsequent chapters of our shared journey unfolded through the enchanting tapestry of the *"Twenty + One"* series. With each page turned, it felt as though a brushstroke was added to the canvas of our collective imagination—stories and sentiments woven to echo within the quiet corners of your heart. These weren't just words; they were invitations to feel, to reflect, and to remember what truly matters.

And how can I not cherish the transformative path we walked together through the *"Life Changing Journey—Inspirational Quotes Series?"* Day by day, quote by quote, we ventured inward—into spaces often overlooked—to find wisdom in simplicity and light in life's shadows. Each reflection was offered as a gentle whisper of hope, a spark meant to uplift, inspire, and remind us that even in silence, the soul speaks.

The release of "Death - Light of Life and the Shadow of Death" promises to shed new light on the timeless mystery of death.

The **Optimum Python Series** is a comprehensive learning pathway designed to empower readers at every stage of their programming journey. It begins with **Series I: Ultimate Guide for Beginners**, which builds a strong and accessible foundation in Python for newcomers. **Series II: Exploring Data Structures and Algorithms** advances into core computer science concepts, strengthening problem-solving skills and coding efficiency.

Building on this, **Series III: Python Power for Data Science** introduces powerful libraries such as NumPy, Pandas, Matplotlib, and Scikit-learn, guiding readers through data manipulation, visualisation, and foundational machine learning techniques. **Series IV:**

Unleashing the Potential of Data Science with Machine Learning Techniques explores advanced models and real-world applications.

This progression continues with **Series V: Optimum: Python Power – Unleashing the Potential of Data Science with Deep Learning Techniques**, and culminates in **Series VI: From Data to Intelligence – The Deep Learning Revolution**, enabling readers to harness the full potential of data-driven innovation. Whether you are a beginner or an advanced learner, this series serves as your complete roadmap to Python mastery and beyond.

Shree Shambav expands his artistic repertoire with *Whispers of Eternity: A Symphony of Soulful Verses*, a heartfelt exploration of the human experience expressed through lyrical depth and timeless reflection. Complementing this, his *Whispers of the Soul: A Journey Through Haiku* distils profound truths into delicate, poignant verses, capturing the fleeting essence of life with elegant simplicity.

Equally evocative, *Whispers of Stillness: Where the Soul Listens Beyond the Noise* offers meditative couplets that invite readers into silence, where wisdom blossoms in the spaces between words. Together, these works illuminate Shambav's versatility and mastery of soulful expression. They invite readers on a transformative journey of self-discovery, weaving a tapestry of emotion, insight, and transcendence that lingers long after the final page is turned.

Building on this success, he continued to enchant audiences with his subsequent albums: HeartStrings, *Melodies of the Heart*, *Driftwood Memories*, *Winds of Change, The Veil and the Waves, Echoes of the Soul, Phoenix Within,* Uncaged, Where Nature Sings, and Wings of Forever. Each album further solidified his place in the world of music, offering a mesmerising collection of tracks that evoke nostalgia, introspection, and heartfelt connection. With every composition, Shree Shambav weaves a musical journey that lingers in the soul long after the final note fades.

Shree Shambav's latest works shine as luminous beacons on the path of self-discovery, mindful living, and spiritual awakening. His writings span a vast spectrum of human experience, each book offering a doorway to transformation. Among his most celebrated titles are Learn to Love Yourself: A Journey of Discovering Inner Beauty and Strength Through 10 Transformative Rules, The Power of Letting Go: Embrace Freedom and Happiness, A Journey of Lasting Peace, and The Entitlement Trap: Get Over It, Get On.

His thought-provoking works include Whispers of a Dying Soul: Unspoken Regrets and Unlived Dreams, Whispers of Silence: Unlocking Inner Power through Stillness, The Power of Words: Transforming Speech,

Transforming Lives, The Art of Intentional Living: Minimalism for a Life of Purpose, and Awakening the Infinite: The Power of Consciousness in Transforming Life.

In The Power of Manifestation: Unlocking the Path from Thought to Reality, Shree Shambav presents a transformative roadmap for turning vision into lived experience, guiding readers from intention to realisation. Beyond the Veil: A Journey Through Life After Death ventures into the profound mystery of existence beyond the physical realm, inviting contemplation on life, transition, and the eternal soul.

His other compelling works include Bonds Beyond Blood: Where Love Builds Bridges and Bonds Defy Lineage, a heartfelt celebration of love that transcends ancestry and form; The Inner Battlefield: Overcoming the Enemies of the Mind and Soul, a powerful guide to mastering inner conflicts and reclaiming mental sovereignty; and A Journey into Spiritual Maturity: 12 Golden Rules for Inner Transformation, which offers timeless wisdom for seekers evolving toward self-mastery and inner awakening.

In The Seeker's Gold: Unlocking Life's Greatest Treasure, he inspires readers to uncover the hidden riches of the soul, while The Law of Attraction: A Soulful Path reveals how to harmonise thought, energy, and intention to create a life aligned with one's highest purpose. His transformative Born to Rise series further empowers readers to embrace growth, clarity, and lasting fulfilment across every dimension of life.

Shree Shambav is also the author of Mastering the Art of Gratitude: A Journey from Acknowledgement to Awakening, a contemplative series on conscious appreciation, and Whispers of a Silent Monk: Poetic Tales of Love, Loss, and Liberation, a lyrical exploration of silence, surrender, and inner freedom.

In addition, his works Journey of the Soul – Karma Unveiled, Unveiling the Enigma, and Death: Light of Life and the Shadow of Death have been translated into Gujarati and Hindi, extending his spiritual insights to a wider audience.

In addition to these works, Shree Shambav has recently ventured into astrology with the release of Astrology Unveiled – Foundations of Ancient Wisdom Series I to XIX, expanding into the realm of metaphysics. These books explore the foundational principles of Vedic astrology, offering readers a rich and practical understanding of this ancient wisdom.

Your unwavering support, enthusiasm to immerse yourself in my writings, and readiness to embark on these journeys with me have been my greatest sources of inspiration. Your input has been a beacon guiding me through the creation process, moulding these stories into containers of passion, emotion, knowledge, and resonance.

As I unveil this new narrative before you, know that your presence, insights, and shared moments have been my companions. The path we have walked together is etched in the annals of my creative evolution, and it's an honour beyond words to have you by my side once more.

Here's to the readers who have illuminated my path with their presence, who have embraced my stories with open hearts, and who have woven themselves into the very fabric of my literary world. Our journey has been a symbiotic dance of writer and reader, a harmony of souls brought together by the magic of storytelling.

With a heart brimming with appreciation and eyes glistening with anticipation, I extend my deepest gratitude for your unwavering support. Thank you for the memories, the shared emotions, and the countless hours spent in the worlds we've crafted together. As we step into this new adventure, let's continue to explore, feel, and discover the boundless horizons that words can unveil.

Warmly,

Shree Shambav

Suggested Reads

ENDORSEMENTS

The God Frequency is not a book that asks to be believed; it asks to be listened to. With rare clarity and depth, Shree Shambav bridges metaphysics, science, nature, and lived ethics into a single, coherent vision of reality. This work does not simplify truth—it makes it intimate. Readers will find here not answers that close inquiry, but insights that awaken responsibility, humility, and wonder. A profound contribution to contemporary spiritual philosophy.

— Apeksha(IT)

About the Author

Shree Shambav is an internationally acclaimed best-selling author, inspirational speaker, artist, philanthropist, life coach, strategist, and entrepreneur. A world record holder, his deep passion for music led him to create soul-stirring albums, drawing inspiration from his celebrated poetry collection, Whispers of Eternity. His profound insights have sparked deep personal transformations, guiding countless individuals toward self-discovery, purposeful living, and authenticity.

With an extraordinary ability to unlock human potential, Shree empowers individuals to break through limitations and embrace their highest selves. His writings, lectures, and compassionate guidance continue to uplift lives, fostering resilience, mindfulness, and personal growth.

Shree Shambav is a 132x best-selling author celebrated for his profound contributions to personal development and spiritual growth.

Shree Shambav's literary journey took flight with the celebrated Journey of Soul - Karma, where he delved into the depths of human experience to unveil profound insights. Garnering recognition through multiple literature awards, his repertoire includes esteemed works, such as the Twenty + One Series, and the enlightening Life Changing Journey – Inspirational Quotes series.

As a distinguished alumnus of the Indian Institute of Management and the National Institute of Technology, Shree Shambav brings a wealth of corporate acumen from his tenure in multinational corporations. His most recent publications, including Unveiling the Enigma, Death - Light of Life and the Shadow of Death, and Optimum – Power Python Series I, Series II, Series III, Series IV, Series V, and Series VI, demonstrate his mastery of both the literary and technical spheres.

Shree Shambav expands his artistic repertoire with *Whispers of Eternity: A Symphony of Soulful Verses*, a heartfelt exploration of the human experience expressed through lyrical depth and timeless reflection. Complementing this, his *Whispers of the Soul: A Journey Through Haiku* distils profound truths into delicate, poignant verses, capturing the fleeting essence of life with elegant simplicity.

Equally evocative, *Whispers of Stillness: Where the Soul Listens Beyond the Noise* offers meditative couplets that invite readers into silence, where wisdom blossoms in the spaces between words. Together, these works illuminate Shambav's versatility and mastery of soulful expression. They invite readers on a transformative journey of self-discovery, weaving a tapestry of emotion, insight, and transcendence that lingers long after the final page is turned.

Building on this success, he continued to enchant audiences with his subsequent albums: HeartStrings, *Melodies of the Heart*, *Driftwood Memories*, *Winds of Change, The Veil and the Waves, Echoes of the Soul, Phoenix Within,* Uncaged, Where Nature Sings, and Wings of Forever. Each album further solidified his place in the world of music, offering a mesmerising collection of tracks that evoke nostalgia, introspection, and heartfelt connection. With every composition, Shree Shambav weaves a musical journey that lingers in the soul long after the final note fades.

Shree Shambav's latest works shine as luminous beacons on the path of self-discovery, mindful living, and spiritual awakening. His writings span a vast spectrum of human experience, each book offering a doorway to transformation. Among his most celebrated titles are Learn to Love Yourself: A Journey of Discovering Inner Beauty and Strength Through 10 Transformative Rules, The Power of Letting Go: Embrace Freedom and Happiness, A Journey of Lasting Peace, and The Entitlement Trap: Get Over It, Get On.

His thought-provoking works include Whispers of a Dying Soul: Unspoken Regrets and Unlived Dreams, Whispers of Silence: Unlocking Inner Power through Stillness, The Power of Words: Transforming Speech, Transforming Lives, The Art of Intentional Living: Minimalism for a Life of Purpose, and Awakening the Infinite: The Power of Consciousness in Transforming Life.

In The Power of Manifestation: Unlocking the Path from Thought to Reality, Shree Shambav presents a transformative roadmap for turning vision into lived experience, guiding readers from intention to realisation. Beyond the Veil: A Journey Through Life After Death ventures into the profound mystery of existence beyond the physical realm, inviting contemplation on life, transition, and the eternal soul.

His other compelling works include Bonds Beyond Blood: Where Love Builds Bridges and Bonds Defy Lineage, a heartfelt celebration of love that transcends ancestry and form; The Inner Battlefield: Overcoming the Enemies of the Mind and Soul, a powerful guide to mastering inner conflicts and reclaiming mental sovereignty; and A Journey into Spiritual Maturity: 12 Golden Rules for Inner Transformation, which offers timeless wisdom for seekers evolving toward self-mastery and inner awakening.

In The Seeker's Gold: Unlocking Life's Greatest Treasure, he inspires readers to uncover the hidden riches of the soul, while The Law of Attraction: A Soulful Path reveals how to harmonise thought, energy, and intention to create a life aligned with one's highest purpose. His transformative Born to Rise series further empowers readers to embrace growth, clarity, and lasting fulfilment across every dimension of life.

Shree Shambav is also the author of Mastering the Art of Gratitude: A Journey from Acknowledgement to Awakening, a contemplative series on conscious appreciation, and Whispers of a Silent Monk: Poetic Tales of Love, Loss, and Liberation, a lyrical exploration of silence, surrender, and inner freedom.

In addition, his works Journey of the Soul – Karma Unveiled, Unveiling the Enigma, and Death: Light of Life and the Shadow of Death have been translated into Gujarati and Hindi, extending his spiritual insights to a wider audience.

In addition to these works, Shree Shambav has recently ventured into astrology with the release of Astrology Unveiled – Foundations of Ancient Wisdom Series I to XVII, expanding into the realm of metaphysics. These books explore the foundational principles of Vedic astrology, offering readers a rich and practical understanding of this ancient wisdom.

Shree Shambav established the Ayur Rakshita Foundation, which is dedicated to promoting boundless growth, universal fraternity, and environmental protection. The charity helps diverse communities while working for societal progress.

To learn more about Shree Shambav and his works, visit his website at www.shambav.org. For information about the Ayur Rakshita Foundation and its initiatives, visit www.shambav-ayurrakshita.org.

Let's Follow him on Social Media: **@shreeshambav**

Main: https://linktr.ee/shreeshambav

Website: https://www.shambav.org/

LinkedIn: https://www.linkedin.com/in/shreeshambav/

Blog: https://blog.shambav.org/

Instagram: https://www.instagram.com/shreeshambav/

YouTube: https://www.youtube.com/@shreeshambav

Amazon: https://www.amazon.com/author/shreeshambav

Goodreads: https://www.goodreads.com/author/show/22367436.Shree_Shambav

PREFACE

A Word Before the Journey

This book was not written to explain God. It was written because explanation had reached its limit.

Across centuries, human beings have spoken endlessly about truth, argued passionately about divinity, and defended beliefs as if they were possessions. Yet beneath all this effort, something essential has often been missed: **that reality does not ask to be conquered by thought, but met with clarity**.

Shree Shambav's vision emerges from this recognition.

The teachings gathered in *The God Frequency* did not arise from academic speculation or theological debate. They emerged from long periods of silence, observation, and lived inquiry—where questions were allowed to ripen rather than be rushed into answers. What is offered here is not doctrine, but distilled seeing; not authority, but resonance.

This book is addressed equally to the spiritual seeker, the questioning mind, and the quiet sceptic. It does not ask you to replace one belief with another, nor does it dismiss science in favour of mysticism. Instead, it invites a deeper honesty: to see where knowledge ends, where assumptions begin, and where direct perception becomes possible again.

You may notice that the language in these pages often moves slowly. This is intentional. Truth, as presented here, is not dramatic—it is precise. It does not overwhelm; it clarifies. At times, the teaching may feel simple, even obvious. At other times, it may quietly unsettle long-held ideas about self, God, nature, and meaning. Both responses are natural. Neither needs resistance.

This work is divided into two volumes, not for complexity, but for spaciousness. The first restores unity by dissolving false separations. The second explores how that unity expresses itself as vibration, impermanence, and becoming. Together, they form a single movement—like inhalation and exhalation—revealing reality not as fragmented truth, but as living coherence.

The reader is not expected to agree with every insight presented here. Agreement is not transformation. What is asked instead is **attention**—the willingness to pause, to sense, and to notice what resonates beyond habit and conditioning. If a passage feels unclear, allow it to remain so. Understanding, in this vision, ripens through presence, not force.

This book will not tell you who to become.

It will not define God for you.

It will not promise certainty.

What it offers is subtler and more enduring: a way of seeing that softens division, a language that points beyond itself, and a reminder that the sacred is not elsewhere—it is the very field in which reading, questioning, and being occur.

May these pages not add to your knowledge alone, but deepen your listening.

The rest is not instruction.

It is an encounter.

With kindest regards,

Shree Shambav

CONTENTS

INTRODUCTION

Listening Before Belief

This book does not begin with answers.

It begins with listening.

Before philosophy, before theology, before science divided reality into names and measurements, there was a quiet intuition shared by mystics, sages, poets, and silent observers across civilisations: **existence is one movement, not many things**. This intuition was never owned by a single culture, nor confined to a single era. It appeared wherever human beings paused long enough to listen beneath thought.

The God Frequency arises from that pause.

Shree Shambav does not present a new belief system, nor does he ask the reader to abandon reason. Instead, he invites a deeper form of inquiry—one that precedes opinion and survives certainty. In these pages, God is not approached as an external authority, a judge, or a distant creator, but as the **living coherence through which all things appear**. Not an object of worship, but the very vibration that allows awareness, matter, and meaning to arise at all.

The phrase *God Frequency* is not metaphorical poetry alone. It points to an experiential truth: that reality is not static substance, but **dynamic resonance**. Everything that exists—stars and stones, breath and thought, love and grief—appears as modulation within a single, indivisible field. Ancient traditions sensed this as the sacred hum beneath existence; modern science glimpses it through fields, waves, and unified theories. Shree Shambav brings these intuitions together, not to reconcile institutions, but to restore **wholeness of perception**.

This book speaks to those who feel that separation is learned, not natural. That ethics should emerge from understanding, not enforcement. That spirituality should deepen intimacy with life, not distance from it. Here, unity is not an abstract ideal or mystical escape—it is revealed as the most practical truth, transforming how one breathes, relates, works, grieves, and loves.

Across two volumes, the journey unfolds gently.

First, through the recognition of **the One Substance**—the dismantling of false divisions between matter and spirit, self and world, God and nature. Then, through the exploration of **frequency, impermanence, and becoming**—how the One expresses itself as many without ever losing its coherence.

You will find no commandments here.

No promised salvation.

No final conclusions.

What you will find is an invitation to look again—at nature, at suffering, at death, at identity, at silence. To notice that beneath all change there is continuity, and beneath all noise there is a song that never began and never ends.

If this book succeeds, it will not convince you of anything.

It will simply help you hear what has always been present.

The rest is not learning.

It is remembering.

Warm regards,

Shree Shambav

PROLOGUE

The Silence Before Sound

Before the first word was spoken, something was already listening.

Not a being, not a mind, not a god waiting to be named—but a still, luminous presence in which sound, form, and meaning would one day appear. Long before questions arose, before the idea of a seeker or a path, there was coherence. Not emptiness, but an unbroken fullness, resting within itself.

This presence did not create the universe as an act of will. It did not stand apart and design existence from a distance. It moved—quietly, inevitably—not outward, but into expression. And in that movement, vibration was born.

Every tradition remembers this moment differently. Some speak of the Word. Some of the Breath. Some of the Cosmic Egg. Some of an endless void trembling into light. Yet beneath all these metaphors lies the same intuition: **existence began not with matter, but with resonance**.

What followed was not chaos, but rhythm.

Stars learned to burn. Rivers learned to flow. Atoms learned to dance. Life learned to listen to itself. And awareness—subtle, alert, self-luminous—began to recognise its own reflection in form. The universe did not merely expand; it *woke up in stages.*

Human beings arrived much later, carrying this ancient vibration within their bones and breath, yet slowly forgetting how to hear it. In the noise of survival, identity, and belief, the original resonance grew faint. God became distant. Nature became object. The self became isolated. What was once felt as unity hardened into separation.

Still, the frequency never disappeared.

It hummed beneath thought. It pulsed beneath emotion. It waited beneath every moment of stillness, wonder, love, and grief. Whenever a human being paused deeply enough—beneath fear, beneath role, beneath story—it revealed itself again. Not as an answer, but as recognition.

This book begins there.

Not with doctrine or argument, but with remembrance. Not with belief, but with listening. The teachings of Shree Shambav do not point toward a new god, a new system, or a new philosophy. They point toward what has always been present—**the silent coherence from which all knowing arises**.

The God Frequency is not something you must attain. It is something you have never left.

To read these pages is not to move forward in time, but to move inward—toward the still point where sound is born, where form dissolves, and where separation loses its authority.

If you listen carefully, you may notice something subtle happening.

The words may fade.

The ideas may loosen.

And in the space that opens, something ancient may begin to hum again.

That hum is not outside you.

It is what you are listening with.

Warm regards,

Shree Shambav

Prelude

An Invitation to Listen

This book does not begin with an argument.

It begins with an invitation.

Before philosophy, before spirituality, before science and scripture divided the world into methods and meanings, there was a simple human capacity: the ability to listen. Not merely with the ears, but with the whole of one's being—with breath, with silence, with attention unburdened by certainty.

Shree Shambav's vision arises from that listening.

Across cultures and centuries, human beings have sensed that beneath the surface of things—beneath matter and motion, beneath thought and emotion—there is an underlying coherence. A subtle order that is not imposed from above, but expressed from within. Some have called it God. Some have called it Nature. Some have called it Truth, Being, Tao, Brahman, or the Ground of Existence. Names differ, but the intuition remains the same: **reality is not fragmented at its source**.

This work names that coherence *the God Frequency.*

Not as a belief to adopt, nor as a doctrine to defend, but as a way of recognising what has always been present. The God Frequency is not separate from the world; it is the silent rhythm by which the world appears. It vibrates as galaxies and atoms, as forests and oceans, as thought and feeling, as birth and death. It is not supernatural. It is *prior to the division between the natural and the sacred.*

Volume One of this work turns the gaze inward and outward at once—toward the metaphysical foundations of existence. It explores the One Substance beneath apparent multiplicity, the indivisibility of matter and consciousness, the living intelligence of nature, and the vibrational fabric of reality itself. It asks not, "What should we believe?" but, "What is already the case, before belief?"

Volume Two continues the same vision into lived experience. If reality is one, how then do we understand destiny and freedom, karma and responsibility, pain and return? How does a human being live ethically—not out of fear, commandment, or reward—but in alignment with the nature of reality itself? Here, the God Frequency is no longer only contemplated; it is *embodied*—as reason, compassion, humility, and love that seeks understanding rather than domination.

These volumes are not meant to be rushed. They are meant to be *entered.* Each chapter is less a conclusion than a doorway—inviting the reader to pause, to notice, to allow perception itself to soften and widen. Agreement is not required. Reverence is not demanded. Only honesty of attention.

You may find moments of clarity here.

You may also find moments of discomfort.

Both are signs of learning.

If, at times, the language feels simple, it is because truth often is.

If, at times, it feels difficult, it is because habits of seeing run deep.

This work does not promise answers that end inquiry.

It offers a way of seeing that keeps inquiry alive—without violence, without division, without despair.

Read slowly.

Listen deeply.

And remember: what these pages point toward is not distant.

It is the very coherence by which you are reading them.

At Kanchipuram

"Creation did not arise to fill a gap. It arose because fullness longed to be seen."

- Shree Shambav.

Even before the sun remembered how to rise—during **Brahma Muhurtam**, that sacred hinge where night loosens its grip and day learns to breathe—the world around **Kanchipuram** rested in a hush so complete it felt intentional, almost prayerful. Darkness still lingered, but it had softened, thinning into a deep indigo blue, like a veil slowly withdrawn. Night was no longer resisting the dawn; it was bowing to it.

The air was cool and alert, carrying the faint scent of damp earth and flowering neem. Even the wind seemed cautious, moving gently so as not to disturb something holy unfolding unseen.

Beneath the ancient **banyan tree**, **Akshaya** and **Vasudeva** sat cross-legged upon the cool, receptive earth. The banyan's aerial roots descended around them like the matted locks of a great ascetic suspended in timeless contemplation. It was more than a tree—it was a witness. Older than memory, older than language, it had watched kingdoms rise and dissolve, prayers whispered and forgotten, seekers arrive with urgency and depart with quiet humility. Within its silence lingered the residue of countless lives—nothing tangible, yet unmistakably present.

The ground beneath them felt alive—not metaphorically, but palpably—subtly pulsing, as though listening back. Without instruction or signal, their eyes closed. Their spines aligned naturally. Breath slowed and deepened, settling into a rhythm older than language, older than thought. They were not *doing* meditation; meditation was remembering them.

The banyan did not merely shade their bodies—it sheltered their remembering.

A few moments later, **Kiran** arrived, his footsteps measured and reverent, as though silence itself were a fragile vessel he wished to enter without fracture. **Vidyarthi** followed—unhurried, grounded—carrying the quiet confidence of one who had already arrived inwardly long before reaching this place. They joined the circle without greeting, without exchange. At that hour, even names felt excessive. Presence alone was sufficient.

Time loosened its grip.

An hour passed—not marked by clocks, but by the dissolving of effort. By the thinning of thought. By that unmistakable inner moment when attention ceases to search and begins to rest. When their eyes finally opened, there was no dramatic return, no rush back into form. What appeared instead was a quiet luminosity—the stillness of inner waters that had settled completely.

It was not happiness. Not bliss.

It was something rarer and truer:

the feeling of being **at home within oneself**.

Their morning walk followed—not as exercise, but as **prayer in motion**. Each step was deliberate, unhurried, as though the earth beneath their feet were sacred scripture and they were reading it line by line. No one spoke. Silence walked with them—not as absence, but as a companion who knew the way.

As they approached the temple grounds, silence did not break.

It transformed.

Bhajans drifted through the air—**tabla** and **dholak** laying down steady heartbeats, the **harmonium** breathing long devotional phrases. **Om** rose and fell, not merely chanted but embodied, rippling through stone, air, and bone alike. Temple bells rang—round and generous—each peal dissolving into the next, as though time itself were being gently awakened.

The fragrance of flowers, sandalwood, and incense moved freely—curling around pillars, brushing skin, settling into breath. Holiness was not imposed here; it was ambient, like oxygen. One did not enter it. One realised they had always been within it.

Nearby, devotees moved through yogic postures—bodies rising and folding like verses written in muscle and breath. Others tended the gardens, hands deep in soil, leaves brushed aside with care. No task felt lesser. Stillness and action were simply two expressions of the same devotion.

Morning in Kanchipuram did not arrive as an ordinary day.

It unfolded—slowly, reverently—like a forgotten hymn remembered by the soul before the mind could claim it.

A cool breeze moved through the temple streets, carrying the scent of last night's rain softened by jasmine. Tiny streams murmured beside stone paths, telling stories that had never required listeners. Leaves held dewdrops like quiet offerings. Birds perched in readiness—not yet singing, but listening.

In the distance, **Aastha, Abhirami, Kiran, Sam, and Akshatha** wandered through **Brindavan Garden**. Flowers swayed as if responding to an unheard raga, petals bending beneath the weight of dew—reluctant to release the night, yet eager for the day.

From the temple steps, **Akshatha, Nita, Lalitha, Rohith, and Sujitha** emerged, their bhajans still echoing softly in their chests. Soon after, **Roopa,**

Kieron, Astyn, Espen, Greta, and Divyani arrived from their yoga practice—bodies warm, breath aligned, eyes clear—each carrying the quiet harmony that arises when breath and being agree.

This was not a gathering.

It was a **remembering**.

The air itself seemed to whisper:

All that you have sought has always been here.

The sun did not rise.

It arrived—like an honoured guest—offering warmth not as command, but as blessing. The sky softened, melting into gold like ghee into flame. The Earth exhaled—long and contented—as footsteps echoed gently. Seekers were arriving not at a place, but at a moment.

Sofia, Bhavya, and Akanksh walked the gravel path—not as wanderers, but as pilgrims responding to a call older than memory. Neem leaves rustled overhead, their sound forming a tanpura drone, tuning the morning itself. Even the banyans seemed to bow inwardly, roots heavy with remembrance, welcoming souls they had known across lifetimes.

Silence accompanied them—not emptiness, but fullness.

A silence that listened.

Then **Aarna** smiled—a small, effortless curve of warmth.

"Shall we begin with coffee?" she asked.

The words landed gently, like a bell rung not to awaken the world, but to invite it closer. Cups of steaming coffee and tea appeared, glowing like small lamps—warmth traveling from palms to hearts.

Birdsong finally rose—slow, devotional—the **alaap** of the morning raga. Sandalwood mingled with neem blossoms. Soft laughter flowed as **Aarna, Dev, and John** joined, their presence light and unforced—sunlight translated into sound.

After a pause that felt complete, **Akanksh** spoke, his voice steady with reverence.

"Guruji will be speaking today about **Singularity**."

Nods moved through the circle—not agreement, but readiness.

A deeper hush followed.

Apeksha lifted her gaze toward the banyan canopy, where sunlight filtered through leaves like liquid gold. When her eyes returned to the circle, something subtle had shifted—as though an unseen door had opened quietly within the day itself.

Before she could speak, **Abhilasha's** voice rose—low, tender, almost a vibration rather than sound.

“Apeksha,” she said softly, “please… tell us a story to begin our day.”

Apeksha remained silent for a long moment.

Not because she was searching for words—but because she was listening to where the story wished to be born.

When she finally spoke, her voice was soft, yet it carried—a voice shaped by remembrance rather than narration.

“Many years ago,” she began, “before Guruji ever spoke of Singularity, before he used the words *frequency* or *one substance*, we were walking with him along the dry riverbed outside Kanchipuram.”

Some shifted closer. Even the birds seemed to lean in.

“It was summer,” she continued. “The river had almost disappeared. What remained were scattered pools of water—isolated, shallow, vulnerable. One of the devotees with us asked Guruji a question that day.”

Apeksha paused.

‘If God is one,’ the devotee had asked, *‘why does life feel so fragmented?’*

“Guruji stopped walking,” she said. “He looked at the riverbed for a long time—long enough that we grew uncomfortable with our own thoughts.”

Then she smiled faintly.

"He asked us to kneel."

A few in the circle unconsciously adjusted their posture, as if remembering something they had never experienced.

"He pointed to one of the remaining pools of water and said:

'Tell me—where does this water begin, and where does it end?'"

"No one answered," Apeksha said. "So he took a stick and gently drew a line in the sand around the pool."

'Now,' Guruji said, *'does the water feel separate—or only contained?'*

A hush moved through the circle beneath the banyan.

"He then walked to another pool a few meters away and drew another circle."

'And this one?' he asked.

'Is it another water—or the same water paused differently?'

Apeksha looked up, her eyes steady.

"Then Guruji did something unexpected. He scraped away the sand between the two pools. Slowly. Patiently."

The listeners could almost hear the sound.

"When the thin channel formed, the water began to move. The two pools touched. And without effort, without announcement, they became one stream."

Apeksha's voice softened.

'Nothing new was added,' Guruji said.

'Nothing was lost. Only a boundary was removed.'

She let the words settle.

"Then he looked at us and said something I have never forgotten:

'You are not separate from God.

You are God—temporarily held by form, memory, and fear.'"

Silence thickened—not heavy, but alive.

Apeksha continued, "That day, Guruji did not explain Singularity. He **showed it**."

She lowered her gaze.

"Later, when someone asked him why suffering exists if everything is one, he replied:

'Because boundaries hurt when they dissolve.'"

No one spoke.

Even the banyan seemed still.

Aarna exhaled—a soft sigh of arrival.

"It's time for Guruji's morning session."

The circle settled.

Kanchipuram's sacred rhythm—of breath, bell, bird, and being—now pulsed fully alive within them, ready to listen, ready to remember.

Note: Hereafter, Shree Shambav will be referred to as 'Guruji' means Master.

Before the First Vibration

"God is not an object of belief; God is the vibration through which belief, doubt, and being all appear."

- Shree Shambav.

Synopsis

This chapter opens in silence rather than explanation, inviting the reader into a space before thought, before form, before time itself. Shree Shambav introduces Singularity not as emptiness or chaos, but as primordial fullness—an undivided coherence from which all existence emerges and into which it continually returns. Across ancient civilisations and spiritual traditions, echoes of this same intuition appear: creation does not arise from lack, but from an overflowing presence. Shree Shambav names this presence the God Frequency—the eternal hum beneath sound, light, and movement. Speaking not as a teacher but as a witness, he reveals that God is neither distant nor external, but the very vibration through which awareness, matter, and life appear. Creation is thus not a single event in the past, but an ongoing remembering of unity taking form. The chapter gently shifts the seeker's gaze inward, inviting a deeper listening—to the silence that is not absence, but the source of all becoming.

All the devotees had settled into **Buddha Hall**, not merely seated, but inwardly arranged.

Spines rose naturally, without stiffness. Breath moved without instruction. Eyes rested in that gentle openness that appears only when effort quietly steps aside. It was not discipline that shaped the room—it was readiness. The hall itself seemed to listen. Its high ceilings held silence the way a bowl holds water—without spilling, without strain.

Minutes passed uncounted.

Then **Guruji entered**.

He did not announce himself. He never did.

His presence arrived the way fragrance does—noticed only after it has already filled the space. A soft smile rested on his face, not aimed at anyone in particular, yet somehow received by all. With folded palms, he offered **Atma Namaskar**—not as greeting, but as recognition. One awareness bowing to itself, appearing as many.

He paused at the centre of the hall.

Then, with effortless grace, he took his **asana**.

The hall exhaled as one body.

Silence settled—soft, fertile, expectant. Not the silence of waiting, but the silence of remembering something just before it arrives.

When Guruji finally spoke, his voice carried neither authority nor insistence. It carried **clarity**, the kind that does not persuade but reveals.

Apeksha's voice rose gently from the stillness.

"Guruji," she asked, "before creation… what existed?"

Shree Shambav did not answer immediately.

He leaned forward slightly, placed his palm upon the earth beneath him, and said softly,

"Listen."

Silence thickened—not as absence, but as presence becoming audible.

Then he began.

Ancient Memories of Before-Beginning

"Across civilisations," Guruji said, "humanity has always tried to remember what came before the first sound."

He did not say *imagine*.

He said *remember*.

Mesopotamia — The Waters Before the Gods

"In the ancient lands of Mesopotamia," he continued, "they spoke of a time before gods themselves were born. There was only **water**—Tiamat, the salt sea, and Apsu, the fresh. Chaos and order were not enemies then; they were indistinguishable currents within the same depth."

He paused.

"Notice this," he said.

"Even chaos was not nothing. It was substance without form."

The devotees listened differently now.

The Vedic Seeing — The Unasked Question

"In the **Rigveda**," Guruji went on, "the sages were more daring. They did not rush to answers. They asked instead:

Was there existence then?

Or was there non-existence?

Who truly knows?"

He smiled faintly.

"They called it **Nasadiya**—the hymn of unknowing. Darkness wrapped darkness. Not emptiness, but potential so complete it had not yet chosen expression.

Then arose **Hiranyagarbha**—the golden womb—not as creation, but as **intention becoming visible**."

A few heads bowed instinctively.

Egypt — The First Rising

"In ancient Egypt," Guruji said, "they remembered **Nun**, the infinite waters. From it arose a small mound—the **Benben**. Not a mountain. Not a palace. Just a place where consciousness could stand and look at itself for the first time."

He tapped the ground lightly.

"Creation does not begin grandly.

It begins precisely."

Genesis — The Hovering

"In the Genesis memory," he continued, "the earth was formless and void. Darkness lay upon the deep. And something hovered—not acted, not commanded—**hovered**."

His voice softened.

"That hovering is important. It is awareness before interference. Presence before decision."

Greece — The Gap

"And the Greeks," he said, "spoke of **Chaos**. Not disorder, as you understand it today, but a vast opening. A gap. A womb without walls."

He looked around the hall.

"Every tradition remembered the same truth differently—because memory bends through culture. But all of them sensed one thing."

He paused.

Then Guruji spoke—not as a teacher, but as one describing something intimately familiar.

"Before sound, before light, before time learned to walk," he said,

"there was **Singularity**."

The word did not land like a concept.

It landed like recognition.

"Not emptiness," he continued, "but fullness beyond measure.
Not disorder, but **perfect coherence**.

Not many things waiting to be arranged—

but **One**, waiting to be known."

He looked at the devotees—not at their faces, but somewhere behind them.

"What you call God," he said gently,

"is not above you."

A stillness passed through the hall.

"It vibrates as you.

This eternal hum—this silent, self-aware fullness—is what I call **God Frequency**."

He rested his palm again on the earth.

"Creation did not begin with sound.

Sound was simply the first ripple noticed."

Shree Shambav fell silent.

No one moved.

No one took notes.

No one searched for meaning.

Meaning was already present.

This was not a lesson about origins.

It was an invitation to **listen beneath thought**—

to sense that even now, beneath breath and heartbeat,

the same coherence hums quietly.

Before creation.

Before identity.

Before seeking.

Still here.

Still vibrating.

Akanksh's question lingered in the hall like a stone dropped into still water. It was not the kind of question that seeks information; it was the kind that trembles at the edge of understanding. Many devotees felt it rise within them too, unspoken until now.

"Guruji," he asked softly, "if fullness existed first, why did creation arise at all?"

Shree Shambav did not respond immediately. He closed his eyes—not in withdrawal, but in remembrance. His breath slowed, and with it, the room seemed to soften. After a long, compassionate pause, he spoke.

"Akanksh," he said gently, "this question carries a very human assumption—that creation must be born from lack, from need, from something missing. We ask *why* only when we believe there was a problem to solve."

He looked around the hall, his gaze resting briefly on each face, as though including everyone in the reply.

"Tell me," he continued, "does a lamp shine because it is dark inside? Does a river flow because it is thirsty? Does a flower bloom because it is incomplete?"

The devotees listened, not with their minds alone.

"Creation did not arise to become whole," Guruji said. "It arose *because it was already whole.* What you call creation is not a repair—it is an expression. Just as music pours out of a musician not because silence is broken, but because silence is rich… existence unfolded not out of necessity, but out of joy."

He picked up a small flower that lay near his asana, holding it between his fingers.

"This flower does not bloom to prove anything," he said. "It blooms because blooming is its nature. In the same way, Singularity did not *decide* to create. There was no moment of intention, no desire, no lack. There was only fullness so complete that it moved—not outward, but inward—into forms."

He placed the flower back on the earth.

"Creation," he said quietly, "is fullness playing hide-and-seek with itself. Nothing was missing. Yet everything appeared. Not to gain something new, but to experience itself from infinite angles."

The hall was silent again, but now the silence felt warmer—like understanding settling gently into the heart.

Akshatha's question arose gently, almost hesitantly, as if she were careful not to disturb the stillness that had already settled in the hall.

"Guruji," she asked, "is silence greater than sound in spiritual life?"

Shree Shambav smiled—not as one who had heard this question many times, but as one who recognises a sincere turning inward. He folded his palms briefly, then rested them on his knees.

"Akshatha," he said softly, "silence is not greater than sound. It is *prior* to sound."

He allowed the words to settle, then continued.

"Before a word is spoken, before a chant is sung, before even a thought forms—there is silence. Sound is not the opposite of silence; it is silence taking shape. Just as waves are not separate from the ocean, sound is not separate from silence."

He tapped his fingers lightly on the floor—once. The soft echo lingered, then dissolved.

"Did you notice?" he asked. "The sound appeared… and where did it go?"

The devotees followed the sound back into stillness.

"In spiritual life," Guruji said, "many believe silence means withdrawal—closing the mouth, escaping the world, rejecting expression. This is a misunderstanding. True silence does not silence life; it *sanctifies* it."

He leaned slightly forward.

"When silence is not understood, words scatter the mind. Actions become noisy. Even prayer turns into a demand. But when silence is known, sound becomes sacred. Words carry weight. Actions arise from clarity. Even a single sentence can become a teaching."

He paused, letting his gaze rest on Akshatha.

"Silence is not muteness," he said. "It is intelligence. It knows when to speak, when to act, and when to simply be. It listens before it moves. It holds before it expresses."

The hall felt deeper now—not quieter, but more alive.

"So do not chase silence by running away from sound," Guruji said. "Instead, discover the silence *within* sound. Then every word becomes prayer, and every action becomes meditation."

Akshatha lowered her eyes, not in humility, but in recognition.

Apeksha's question did not break the silence—it rose *from* it.

"Guruji," she asked, her voice steady yet tender, "how do we attune ourselves to the God Frequency?"

Shree Shambav's eyes softened, as though he were looking not at her alone, but at something ancient stirring behind her words. A slow smile appeared—one that carried neither instruction nor mystery, but recognition.

"Apeksha," he said gently, "attunement is not achieved through effort, belief, or ritual alone. It happens through listening."

He paused, letting the word *listening* open rather than define itself.

"Not listening with the ears," he continued, "but with the whole being. When the mind stops forcing meaning… when the breath returns to its own natural rhythm… when identity loosens its grip on who it insists you are—then the original vibration becomes perceptible."

The hall seemed to lean inward.

"The God Frequency is not something you enter," Guruji said. "It is something you remember. It has always been present—beneath thought, beneath fear, beneath the sense of separation. It waits not for achievement, but for stillness."

He closed his eyes briefly, then opened them again.

"Let me tell you a story."

The Story of the Veena and the Silent String

"There was once a master veena maker who crafted instruments so precise that even the air around them seemed to listen. One day, a young disciple came to him, troubled.

'Master,' the disciple said, 'I have learned all the ragas. My fingers are strong, my knowledge complete. Yet when I play, something essential is missing. The music feels correct—but not alive.'

The master said nothing. He handed the disciple a veena and asked him to play.

The notes were flawless. The rhythm exact. Still, the master shook his head.

Then the master did something unexpected. He removed one string—not the one meant to be played, but the string that rests beneath, rarely touched, almost invisible.

'Play again,' the master said.

The disciple tried. The music collapsed.

Confused, he asked, 'Why remove a string that is never played?'

The master replied, 'That string was never meant to be struck. It was meant to *listen*. Without it, the other strings lose their depth. It does not make sound, yet it holds the music together.'

The disciple sat in silence. For the first time, he noticed the space between notes—the pause, the resonance, the unseen harmony that allowed sound to become music.

The master smiled. 'You have been trying to *produce* music,' he said. 'Music happens when you are tuned to what already vibrates.'"

Guruji's gaze returned to the circle.

"You are that silent string," he said softly. "When you stop trying to become spiritual, when you stop striking yourself with effort, the resonance returns. Life begins to play through you."

The devotees sat unmoving, breath slow, awareness wide.

"This," Guruji said, "is attunement. Not becoming divine—but remembering that you never left the rhythm."

Silence followed—not as an ending, but as a completion.

And in that silence, something within everyone subtly aligned—

as if the universe itself had been gently tuned back to its original key.

PART ONE

THE ONE SUBSTANCE

"Difference is how the One moves; separation is how the mind freezes that movement."

- *Shree Shambav*

CHAPTER I

The Myth of Many

"Multiplicity is not the truth of existence—it is the echo of a fractured way of seeing."

– Shree Shambav.

Synopsis

This chapter reveals duality not as a cosmic truth, but as a habit of perception shaped by fear and survival. Through Shree Shambav's teaching and the parable of the broken mirror, multiplicity is shown to be an appearance arising from fragmented seeing, not from fragmented reality. The universe is not a collection of separate things but a single, indivisible movement of the One—expressing itself as form, life, and consciousness. Shree Shambav gently dismantles the false split between matter and spirit, God and nature, soul and body, restoring wholeness to everyday existence. Unity is not presented as an abstract idea or mystical escape, but as a living recognition that transforms how one breathes, acts, and relates. When perception heals, ethics arise naturally, fear loosens its grip, and life is lived as participation rather than opposition. Oneness is not attained—it is remembered, and in that remembering, the world is reclaimed as sacred.

After the coffee break, the devotees returned to Buddha Hall—not with the restlessness of bodies resuming a session, but with the quiet ripeness of minds that had steeped in silence. Conversations had been few, smiles gentle, eyes reflective. Something had already begun working within them, unseen. Now the hall waited again, as if it had never stopped listening.

Guruji entered without sound.

He took his seat slowly. The pause that followed was long—not awkward, not empty. It was the kind of pause that allows truth to arrive without being pushed. When he finally spoke, his voice was soft, almost conversational, yet it carried the weight of something fundamental.

"Let me narrate a tale," he said.

The hall leaned in.

The Broken Mirror

"A child was playing in his room," Guruji began, "running, laughing, alive in that effortless joy children know. In his play, he struck a mirror. It shattered—

glass scattering across the floor, reflections multiplying instantly."

Guruji lifted his hand gently, as if the shards were still falling.

"The child looked down and began to cry. Everywhere he saw himself—dozens of faces, broken, distorted, fragmented. He panicked. 'I am broken,' he wept. 'There are so many of me, and they are all shattered.'"

A hush deepened.

"The mother rushed in. She did not scold him. She did not rush to clean the glass. She knelt beside him and asked a single question."

Guruji paused, letting the question arrive before the words.

"'Did you break yourself,' she asked, 'or did you only break the glass?'"

Silence settled like dew.

Guruji looked around the hall, his gaze steady, compassionate.

"This," he said softly, "is the story of humanity."

He let the words breathe.

"Human suffering begins with division—matter versus spirit, God versus nature, soul versus body. We believe we are broken because the mirror of perception has fractured. We mistake reflections for reality. We count pieces and forget the face."

His voice carried no accusation—only clarity.

"You think the body is separate from the soul. You think nature is outside God. You think the universe is something created *by* God, as if divinity stood apart, supervising from a distance."

He shook his head gently.

"This is the fundamental misunderstanding."

One Appearing as Many

"There are not many things," Guruji said after a pause. "There is only One—appearing as many."

The words landed not as philosophy, but as recognition.

"The universe is not made *of* God," he continued. "It *is* God in motion. Every atom is not carrying God—it is participating in God. Every breath is not reaching toward the divine—it is the divine breathing itself."

The hall felt suddenly intimate, as though walls had softened.

"When you divide, suffering is born. When you reunite, peace is remembered. The body is not the enemy of spirit. Nature is not separate from the sacred. Your thoughts are not outside the divine field—they arise within it."

He leaned forward slightly.

"Just as the child was never broken—only the mirror—so you have never been divided. Only your way of seeing has fractured."

The Return to Wholeness

Guruji closed his eyes briefly, then opened them.

"When this understanding dawns," he said, "something extraordinary happens. Fear loosens. Guilt dissolves. The need to escape the world fades. You stop trying to reach God—and begin living as participation."

He smiled faintly.

"You stop asking, 'How do I become whole?' because you see—you never stopped being whole."

Another pause followed, deep and complete.

Then, softly, almost as a whisper meant for the heart rather than the mind, Guruji said once more:

"There are not many things—there is only One appearing as many."

No one moved.

Somewhere inside, a mirror quietly fell away—

and what remained was not reflection,

but presence.

Abhilasha's question carried a quiet urgency, as if it had been forming long before words gave it shape.

"Guruji," she asked, "why does the mind insist on division?"

Shree Shambav closed his eyes for a brief moment, not to search for an answer, but to allow the question to settle into its proper depth. When he opened them, his gaze was gentle, almost parental.

"Abhilasha," he said softly, "the mind was never created to reveal truth. It was shaped to preserve life."

The hall leaned inward.

"In the earliest days of humanity," Guruji continued, "the mind learned to survive by dividing. This is danger, this is safety. This is food, this is threat. This is mine, this is not. Division was necessary. Without it, the body would not have lived long enough to ask questions about the soul."

He paused, letting the practicality of the mind be honoured rather than condemned.

"But survival," he said, "is not the same as reality."

He gestured gently, as if opening an ancient book in the air.

"In the Upanishads, there is a story of the One who wished to know itself. It is said: *'Ekam eva advitiyam'*—the One without a second. Yet the same text later speaks of the many. Not because the One truly became divided, but because perception narrowed. When sight is whole, there is One. When sight contracts, there are many."

He smiled faintly.

"The mind is that contraction."

Guruji then offered another image.

In the *Brihadaranyaka Upanishad*, this moment unfolds not as a cold philosophical claim, but as an intimate farewell between two souls.

Yajnavalkya , preparing to renounce worldly life, turns to his wife Maitreyi—not to console her with sentiment, but to offer her the rarest gift: clarity. Maitreyī does not ask for wealth or security; she asks a far deeper question: *"Will possessions make me immortal?"* In that single inquiry, she reveals her hunger is not for comfort, but for truth.

Yajnavalkya answers gently yet unflinchingly. He tells her that a husband is not loved for the husband's sake, nor a wife for the wife's sake, nor children, wealth, or gods for their own sake. All are loved for the sake of the Self (*Atman*). This is not a dismissal of love—it is its unveiling.

What he points to is the hidden architecture of affection. The mind experiences love as division: *I love you; you complete me; you belong to me.* But wisdom sees otherwise. What we truly seek in another is the echo of our own being—the sense of fullness, continuity, and aliveness that arises when the Self recognises itself. The beloved becomes a mirror in which consciousness glimpses its own joy.

Yajnavalkya is not saying love is selfish. He is saying love is *non-dual.* The error lies in mistaking the form for the source. When the form changes—as all forms must—suffering is born. But when one sees that the same life breathes through self and other alike, love is freed from fear, possession, and loss.

Thus, love is not two reaching toward each other in need; it is one life delighting in its own reflection across many faces. To know the Self, Yajnavalkya tells Maitreyi, is to know everything—and to love without clinging. In that knowing, love does not end with separation; it becomes boundless, because it no longer depends on any single form to exist.

Abhilasha listened, her eyes moist with recognition.

"The mind names," Guruji continued. "It categorises. It separates. And in doing so, it creates boundaries. Boundaries give control, and control gives a sense of safety. But this safety is borrowed. It costs us wholeness."

He leaned forward slightly.

"Imagine a river that begins to fear the ocean. To protect itself, it builds walls and calls itself separate. For a while, it feels secure. But soon it stagnates. The river suffers not because it is wrong, but because it has forgotten its movement."

The devotees sat still, breathing the metaphor in.

"Division is not a flaw," Guruji said gently. "It is a function. Suffering begins only when we mistake this function for reality—when we believe the map is the territory, when we confuse labels for life."

He lifted his hand, palm open.

"Spiritual maturity does not destroy the mind. The Gita never asks Arjuna to abandon his intellect. Krishna asks him to *see rightly*. The mind must be placed back in service—not of fear, but of unity."

His voice softened.

"When the mind serves fear, it divides the world. When it serves truth, it becomes a bridge. It still names, still distinguishes—but it no longer forgets the One beneath the many."

A deep stillness followed.

Abhilasha lowered her head—not in submission, but in relief. She had not been asked to fight her mind. She had been invited to place it gently back where it belonged.

And in that moment, division loosened—not as an enemy defeated, but as a tool finally understood.

Roopa's question rose from a place deeper than curiosity. It carried the quiet ache of someone who had understood much, yet longed to *be* what she understood.

"Guruji," she asked, "can unity be lived, or only understood?"

Shree Shambav looked at her for a long moment, not measuring her words, but listening to the space behind them. Then he spoke, slowly, as one laying stones across a river.

"Roopa," he said, "unity is incomplete if it remains an idea."

A few heads lifted. A few breaths deepened.

"To understand unity," he continued, "is like seeing the ocean from a hilltop. You know it is vast. You know it is real. But your feet are still dry. To live unity is to step into the water and allow it to change how you walk."

He let the image settle.

Guruji paused before speaking, as though allowing the silence itself to prepare the teaching.

"In the Upanishads," he began, "there is the story of Shvetaketu and his father Uddalaka—one of the most tender and exacting lessons ever given from parent to child."

Shvetaketu had returned home after years of study, proud of his learning, sharp in speech, confident in his intellect. His mind was full of names, categories, and conclusions. Uddalaka saw this and did not rebuke him. Instead, he chose demonstration over argument—experience over explanation.

One evening, Uddalaka placed a lump of salt into a bowl of water and asked his son to leave it overnight. By morning, the salt had vanished. "Bring me the salt," the father said. Shvetaketu searched the vessel carefully. There was nothing to grasp, nothing to point to. "It is gone," he replied.

"Then taste the water," Uddalaka instructed.

Shvetaketu tasted from one side. "Salty."

"From the middle?"

"Salty."

"From the far side?"

"Salty."

The salt could not be seen, yet it was present everywhere—permeating the water without form, without boundary.

Uddalaka then spoke the words that would echo through the centuries: **"Tat Tvam Asi."** *That Thou Art.*

He was not speaking of belief, nor offering poetry. He was revealing the nature of reality. Just as salt dissolves and becomes inseparable from water, the Self dissolves into all existence. It cannot be isolated, named, or possessed. You cannot point to it and say, *Here it is.* Yet wherever you touch life—thought, breath, body, world—it is there, unmistakable.

Shvetaketu had been searching for truth as an object, something to acquire through effort and intelligence.

His father showed him that truth is not found by grasping, but by tasting—by direct awareness. What you seek is not elsewhere. It is the very essence by which you seek.

"Tat"—that vast, unseen reality behind all forms. "Tvam"—you, the one who wonders, doubts, and searches.

"Asi"—are.

Not *will become*. Not *must attain*. **Are.**

The lesson was both humbling and liberating. The divine is not distant. It is closer than breath, subtler than thought, present in every experience yet untouched by any. To know this is not to inflate the ego, but to dissolve it—just as salt dissolves into water, losing form but gaining infinity.

Guruji smiled softly. "When you stop trying to find the salt," he said, "and begin to taste the water of your own being, the teaching reveals itself. You have never been separate. You have only been forgetting."

And in that remembering, the search ends—not because the truth has been captured, but because the seeker has finally recognised himself everywhere.

He turned gently toward Roopa.

"Understanding is knowing the salt is there. Living is tasting the water in everything."

The hall was silent, attentive.

"When unity is only understood," Guruji said, "it remains a philosophy. It may calm the mind, but it does not transform the heart. But when unity is lived, something radical happens."

He raised his hand slightly.

"Compassion becomes spontaneous. You do not decide to be kind—you simply cannot be cruel. Exploitation feels absurd, like cutting your own hand to feed your mouth. Reverence enters ordinary acts—washing dishes, speaking to a stranger, touching the earth."

He smiled softly.

Guruji then told a quiet story.

"There was once a sage who realised the Self and withdrew into the forest. Years later, a villager found him and said, 'If you have realised oneness, why do you live alone?' The sage returned to the village. From that day onward, he drew water, tended children, healed animals, and listened to grief. Someone asked him, 'Are you still in oneness?' He replied, 'Now more than ever—because now there is no one left to avoid.'"

A few devotees smiled. A few wiped their eyes.

"Unity lived," Guruji said, "is not mystical fireworks. It is how you speak when you are tired. How you act when no one is watching. How gently you treat what you once called 'other.'"

Roopa bowed her head—not to Guruji, but to the quiet recognition stirring within her.

Unity had not asked her to leave the world.

It had asked her to enter it fully.

Akshaya's question came not from fear, but from tenderness—an unspoken concern that in touching the infinite, something intimate might be lost.

"Guruji," he asked quietly, "does individuality disappear in oneness?"

Guruji looked at him with a warmth that felt almost protective. He smiled, as one smiles at a child afraid that growing up might mean losing the self.

"Akshaya," he said, "individuality does not disappear. It is purified."

He lifted his hand and drew a slow curve in the air.

"Just as a wave does not vanish when it knows it is the ocean, a person does not dissolve into nothingness upon realising oneness. The wave still rises, still dances, still has its own height and rhythm. What disappears is not the wave—but the belief that it was ever separate from the ocean."

The devotees sat very still.

Guruji continued, his voice calm but edged with quiet insistence.
"When rivers enter the sea, they lose their names. This is where people misunderstand the teaching. They imagine annihilation—an ending, a loss. But look more carefully. Tell me: does the water vanish, or does it finally escape all boundaries?

The river was confined to a course, a history, a direction. It was known as *this* and not *that*. But in the ocean, the same water is no longer trapped in a single identity. It rises as cloud, falls as rain, moves as current, touches every shore. What was once limited becomes limitless.

Nothing is destroyed. Only the illusion of separateness dissolves.

"So it is with the Self," Guruji said softly. "Names fall away, not existence. Form relaxes, not life. What ends is not being, but the idea of being only one thing."

He paused, letting the words settle.

"Freedom is not disappearance," he said. "It is belonging everywhere."

He paused, allowing the question to ripple.

"What is lost is only the boundary, not the essence."

"In the Gospel of John, it is written: *'I and the Father are one.'* Yet Jesus still speaks, walks, weeps, heals. Oneness did not erase his individuality—it freed it from fear. His actions flowed from belonging, not from self-protection."

A few devotees exchanged glances, sensing the bridge between traditions.

"When individuality is rooted in separation," Guruji said, "it is fragile. It must defend itself, compare itself, assert itself. This is ego. Ego is not individuality—it is individuality afraid of disappearing."

He leaned slightly forward.

"But when individuality is rooted in oneness, it becomes fearless. Expression without ego. Form without anxiety. Uniqueness without isolation."

Guruji after a pause said, "There was once a lamp afraid of the sunrise. 'If the sun comes,' it thought, 'I will disappear.' But when dawn arrived, the lamp did not vanish—it was simply no longer needed. Its light had not failed; it had fulfilled its purpose."

The hall felt luminous now.

"Oneness," Guruji said softly, "does not erase you. It releases you—from the burden of having to be separate."

Akshaya's shoulders relaxed. What he feared losing, he realised, had never truly been his.

And what remained felt wider, truer, and strangely more intimate than before.

CHAPTER II

The God Particle

"Infinity learned to whisper—and matter appeared."

– Shree Shambav.

Synopsis

This chapter introduces the God Particle not as a physical fragment to be isolated, but as the metaphysical singular substance from which all form, motion, and awareness arise. Shree Shambav reveals that reductionism fails not because science is wrong, but because reality is indivisible. The smallest particle is shown to be infinite—not by size, but by source. Stars, thoughts, emotions, pain, and love are understood as different gestures of the same self-caused substance. Through ancient insights and lived awareness, the chapter bridges mysticism and modern inquiry, showing that what science approaches through measurement, spirituality encounters through presence. Suffering is reframed as a localised contraction of perception within perfection, not a flaw in existence itself. The God Particle is not something to be found elsewhere—it is the very ground of experience, silently sustaining all that appears. To recognise it is not to escape the world, but to see the world as sacred motion.

After the midday meal—simple, nourishing, shared in quiet gratitude—the rhythm of the ashram softened. Conversations moved gently, like streams that know where they are going and feel no need to rush. Laughter arose, then dissolved. A brief rest followed, not as sleep but as surrender, allowing the body to settle back into its natural intelligence.

When the seekers returned to the Buddha Hall, they did not *enter* it—they *rejoined* it.

Their footsteps were lighter now, instinctively careful, as though the floor itself were a living manuscript. Cushions were adjusted with mindfulness, shawls drawn around shoulders, not for warmth but for inwardness. Spines aligned without instruction. Breath slowed of its own accord. Thoughts loosened, like knots that untie when they realize they are no longer needed.

The air waited.

Silence did not fall; it ripened. It thickened into presence—dense, luminous, listening. No one spoke, yet everyone was attentive, as though the hall had become a single inhalation held gently, without strain.

After some minutes, Guruji entered.

As always, he did not announce himself. His presence was felt the way twilight is felt—before color changes, before stars appear. He bowed slightly, not to the people, but to the stillness that already existed. Then he took his seat.

Then Guruji spoke. His voice was calm, measured, luminous—carrying neither authority nor demand, only clarity.

Padma broke the silence gently.

"Guruji," she asked, "what is the smallest particle?"

Guruji reached down, lifted a single grain of sand from the floor, and held it between his fingers. The gesture was simple, almost playful.

"This," he said, "contains galaxies."

A soft ripple moved through the hall—not of surprise, but of recognition.

He placed the grain back on the earth and paused, allowing the mind to stumble where it needed to.

"There is only one particle," Guruji continued, "eternal, infinite, self-caused, self-sustaining. Science touches its shadow; mysticism lives its pulse."

He looked slowly across the circle.

"Do not mistake this for the Higgs alone, or any named particle. Names belong to perception. What I speak of is the substance beneath all substances—the singular reality from which matter, energy, thought, and feeling arise."

He leaned slightly forward.

"Stars are its gestures. Thoughts are its whispers. Pain is its compression. Love is its recognition."

The hall felt vast now, as though distance itself had folded inward.

"In the Upanishads," Guruji said, "it is written: *'That which is smaller than the smallest and greater than the greatest dwells in the heart of all beings.'* The mind hears this and searches outward. The wise hear it and become still."

Anoraniyaan mahato mahiyaan atma'sya jantor nihito guhayaam |

Tam akratuh paśyati vitasoko dhatuh prasadan mahimanam ātmanah ||

Meaning:

"The Self, smaller than the smallest and greater than the greatest,

dwells hidden in the heart of every being.

One who is free from desire and sorrow beholds

the glory of the Self through inner clarity."

Guruji said, "This verse reveals the paradox at the heart of non-dual wisdom: the Absolute is infinitely subtle yet infinitely vast—immanent within the heart of every being, and at the same time beyond all measure. This is what I point to as the God Frequency—dwelling silently within all forms, untouched by size, distance, or time."

He smiled gently.

"In the Buddhist texts," Guruji said, "there is a quiet teaching that often escapes the hurried mind. It is said that within a single mustard seed exist innumerable worlds."

He paused and looked at the floor, as though the seed itself were resting there.

"To the ordinary eye, a mustard seed is insignificant—easily lost, easily crushed. But the Buddha did not speak to the eye alone. He spoke to perception purified of division."

He lifted his gaze.

"When the mind fragments reality, size becomes absolute—this is small, that is vast. But when fragmentation dissolves, scale collapses. The smallest no longer excludes the infinite."

He let the words settle, then continued with a story.

"There was once a monk who asked his teacher, 'How can the universe fit into a mustard seed?' The teacher placed the seed in the monk's palm and asked, 'Does the sky fit into your eye?' The monk laughed. The teacher said, 'And yet you see it.'"

A gentle stillness moved through the hall.

"The universe is not *contained* in the seed the way water is contained in a pot," Guruji clarified. "It is present the way reflection is present—without weight, without crowding. The mustard seed does not *hold* worlds; it *expresses* the same reality that forms worlds."

Guruji sensed that the image had touched something, yet its depth still waited to be unfolded. He spoke again, not to add complexity, but to dissolve confusion.

"In the *Avatamsaka Sutra*," he said, "Indra's Net is not offered as poetry alone—it is a map of perception when separation dissolves."

He paused, then began slowly.

"Imagine an infinite net, without beginning or end, stretching across all existence. There is no centre and no edge. At every crossing of the threads hangs a luminous jewel. Each jewel is perfectly clear, without dust, without distortion."

He lifted his hand slightly, as if holding one.

"Now look into a single jewel. You will see every other jewel reflected within it. And if you look into one of those reflections, you will again see the entire net—reflected endlessly, without loss, without repetition."

The hall was utterly still.

"This image is meant to break the mind's habit of linear thinking," Guruji said. "The mind asks, 'Which came first? Which is more important? Which contains which?' Indra's Net answers: *nothing stands alone, and nothing is secondary*."

He leaned forward.

"Each jewel represents a being, a moment, a particle, a thought. The threads represent relationship—not connection added later, but relationship as the very structure of existence."

He let the words breathe.

"You do not exist first and then relate to the universe. You exist *as* relationship."

A quiet recognition moved through the listeners.

"This is why harming another reverberates everywhere. This is why compassion heals more than one life. When one jewel vibrates, the entire net shimmers."

He softened his voice.

"The net is not held together by force, law, or command. It is held together by reflection—by mutual presence. Nothing blocks anything else. Everything participates in everything."

He said gently:

"When reality is seen through fragmentation, we see isolated jewels and call it a broken world. When reality is seen whole, we see Indra's Net—and realise the world has never been divided."

No one moved.

The image had stopped being a concept.

It had become a way of seeing.

He traced a small circle in the air.

"There is no central jewel. No privileged point. Each point is complete. Each part contains the whole—not by possession, but by resonance."

The devotees sat very still, breathing carefully, as if afraid to disturb the vision forming within them.

"This," Guruji said softly, "is reality seen without fragmentation. When the mind stops breaking existence into separate pieces, the universe reveals itself as holographic. Every moment mirrors all moments. Every being carries the signature of the whole."

He smiled faintly.

"Science approaches this through fractals and holograms. Mysticism lives it directly. The difference is not in truth, but in intimacy."

He said gently:

"These are not metaphors of imagination. They are descriptions of what remains when the mind stops dividing. When perception becomes whole, the infinite is no longer elsewhere—it is intimate, immediate, and quietly present in the smallest of things."

The hall felt vast and intimate at once.

A mustard seed lay somewhere in the world—unchanged, unnoticed—yet now known as a doorway.

And no one felt the need to ask another question.

He paused again, then added softly:

"A wave forgets the ocean only while rising."

The words hung in the air, luminous and complete.

“When consciousness rises into identity,” Guruji said, “it feels separate, small, afraid. When it rests, it remembers the ocean it has always been. The smallest particle is not small. It only appears so when seen through division.”

No one moved.

Padma lowered her eyes, not in humility, but in awe. The grain of sand remained on the floor—unchanged, unnoticed by the world, yet now known as infinite.

And in that knowing, the hall itself seemed to breathe—vast, indivisible, alive.

Vasudeva’s question arose with the calm precision of someone who had walked long in both worlds—reason and reverence.

“Guruji,” he asked, “is this particle measurable or experiential?”

Shree Shambav smiled, not because the question was simple, but because it was *ripe*. He let a moment of silence stretch, as if inviting the question to look at itself.

“Vasudeva,” he began gently, “to measure is to stand apart. To experience is to enter.”

He held his palms facing each other, a small distance apart.

"Measurement requires separation—an observer here, an object there. A ruler needs two ends. A scale needs distance. But the God Particle is not an object *in* the universe. It is the substance *of* the universe. Where will you stand to measure that which you are standing in?"

A few soft nods moved through the hall.

"In the Upanishads," Guruji continued, "it is said: *'Yena manasa na manute'*—that which the mind cannot think, but by which the mind thinks. This is not poetry. It is a precise statement. You cannot turn the source into an object without losing it."

Guruji's voice softened, as though he were not merely telling a story but reopening an ancient silence.

"Let me narrate a story," he said.

"There is a tale in the *Kena Upanishad*—subtle, luminous, and unsettling in its simplicity.

Once, the gods won a great victory. Darkness was pushed back, chaos subdued, order restored. Thunder echoed their triumph, and the heavens rang with celebration. Each god believed, quietly or openly, *I am the reason*. Agni thought, *It was my fire*. Vayu believed, *It was my force*. Indra felt, *It was my command*. Victory, like sweet wine, made them forget the source from which their power flowed.

At that very moment, the Absolute appeared before them—not as a god, not as a form they could name, but as a strange, silent presence. It did not announce itself. It did not shine or roar. It simply *was*.

The gods were uneasy. Something about this presence disturbed them—not with fear, but with a deeper unease: the feeling of standing before something immeasurable.

They sent Agni first, the proud bearer of fire, the one who could consume forests and offerings alike.

Agni approached and demanded, 'Who are you?'

The presence did not answer. Instead, it placed a single blade of grass before him and asked gently, 'If you are fire, burn this.'

Agni summoned all his power. Flames leapt, heat surged—but the grass did not blacken, did not curl, did not even warm. Agni strained, astonished, humiliated. For the first time, fire met something it could not touch. He withdrew, silent.

Next came Vayu, the god of wind, swift and unstoppable.

'Who are you?' Vayu asked.

Again, no reply. The same blade of grass lay there. 'If you are wind,' the presence asked, 'move it.'

Vayu gathered his might. Storms howled. Invisible force rushed forward—but the grass remained still, unmoved, unbothered. Vayu felt his power collapse inward. He too stepped back, shaken.

Finally, Indra, king of the gods, approached—not with arrogance now, but with hesitation. And before he could speak, the presence vanished.

In its place appeared Uma, the radiant embodiment of wisdom. Through her, Indra understood what the others could not.

The victory was never theirs.

The power they wielded was not owned, only *borrowed.*

Fire burns because the Absolute allows it to burn. Wind moves because the Absolute moves through it. Strength acts only because consciousness breathes through strength.

Without humility, power becomes blind. Without awareness, ability becomes illusion.

Guruji paused, letting the story settle like dust in sunlight.

"This," he said softly, "is the lesson hidden in the tale. The Absolute—the God Particle, if you wish to call it that—cannot be confronted by force, measured by ability, or grasped by pride. The moment you try to dominate it, it disappears. The moment you become empty enough to listen, it reveals itself.

Agni and Vayu failed not because they were weak, but because they assumed separation: *I am here, it is there.* Indra glimpsed the truth only when the question shifted from conquest to understanding.

The Absolute is not impressed by power.

It is revealed by humility.

Just as the blade of grass contained a mystery greater than fire and wind, the smallest moment of awareness contains the whole universe. And just as the gods had to unlearn their pride to see, so must we unlearn our need to measure, label, and control.

The truth does not yield to effort.

It yields to surrender."

Guruji looked at Vasudeva.

"The Absolute could not be *used*, *tested*, or *measured*. It could only be recognised."

He paused, "In the Gospel **Luke 17:21**, Jesus says, 'The Kingdom of God is within you.' He does not say it is to be discovered like land, or measured like grain. He speaks of intimacy, not distance."

A quiet depth filled the room.

"Science," Guruji said warmly, "does something extraordinary. It traces expressions—energy, mass, vibration, fields. It listens to echoes. It studies the handwriting of the One. Mysticism does something equally necessary—it recognises the writer."

He smiled softly.

"Measurement approaches from the outside. Experience meets from within. One maps the riverbanks. The other steps into the water."

He leaned slightly forward.

"When science forgets humility, it believes the map is the land. When mysticism forgets clarity, it rejects the map altogether. Both become incomplete."

His voice softened.

"But when measurement bows to mystery, and experience respects reason, the God Particle is not argued about—it is lived."

Vasudeva lowered his gaze. The question had not been answered in one direction.

It had been completed.

Kiran's question lingered in the air long after it was spoken, like a bell whose echo refuses to fade.

"Guruji," he asked softly, "how does suffering arise from perfection?"

Guruji did not answer at once. He picked up a small crystal lying on the table—clear, unremarkable, almost forgotten. Holding it up to the morning sun, he let the light pass through. A spectrum spilled onto the earth: red, blue, violet, gold.

Then he spoke.

"Perfection does not eliminate suffering," Guruji said. "It contains it. What you call suffering is not born from imperfection, but from *partial seeing.*"

He gestured to the colours on the ground.

"Light itself is whole, indivisible, stainless. Yet when it passes through a prism, it fractures into many colours. None of the colours are false. None are wrong. But if red believes it is only red, it will mourn the loss of blue. If blue clings to itself, it will fear the coming of violet. Suffering begins not when light breaks—but when a fragment forgets it was once whole."

Kiran listened, his eyes fixed on the trembling spectrum.

Guruji continued.

Guruji's smile lingered, and with it, a quiet remembrance began to move through the hall—unspoken, yet unmistakable.

Purnam adah purnam idam

purnat purnam udacyate

purnasya purnam adaaya

purnam evavaśisyate.

Meaning

That is whole; this is whole.

From wholeness, wholeness arises.

When wholeness is taken from wholeness,

wholeness alone remains.

Not as a chant, not as sound, but as recognition.

From fullness, fullness arises. From the infinite, the infinite flows forth. Even when the infinite appears to divide itself, nothing is diminished. Fullness alone remains.

In that light, the question of pain softened. Creation had not torn itself away from wholeness; it had stepped into expression. Infinity had not lost itself—it had leaned closer to itself. What feels like fracture is only fullness learning texture. What feels like suffering is completeness encountering boundaries. The One had not become less by becoming many; it had become intimate.

Guruji's silence held this truth gently. Reality was complete at every level—before form, within form, beyond form. Nothing was missing. And yet, within this perfection, experience unfolded—sharp, tender, luminous—because infinity, unburdened by lack, chose to know itself from the inside.

Guruji closed his eyes for a moment, as if listening to something far older than memory. Then he spoke.

"Let me narrate a story—not as history, but as remembrance.

In the *Brihadaranyaka Upanishad*, there is a subtle insight, almost whispered rather than proclaimed. It says that in the beginning, there was only the One. Not one among many—only One, without a second. Complete. Infinite. Lacking nothing.

Yet the text does not say the One was lonely in the human sense. There was no sadness, no ache, no incompleteness. The One was whole beyond imagination. But within that wholeness arose a gentle stirring—not desire, not need, but *wonder*. A question without words: *'What am I?'*"

Guruji opened his eyes.

"That moment of self-awareness was the first movement. Not a fall, not a fracture—an awakening within fullness itself. Like a mirror discovering it can reflect."

He continued softly.

"The One did not split because it was insufficient. It expressed itself because it was abundant. Just as a dancer dances not because she lacks stillness, but because stillness overflows into motion."

He paused, letting the image settle.

"But the moment the One said—even silently—*'I am'*, there arose the faintest shadow of *'that'*. Subject and object. Seer and seen. This was the birth of two—not in reality, but in perception."

Guruji traced a line in the dust with his finger.

"And where there are two, comparison begins. One seems nearer, another farther. One brighter, another dimmer. Comparison is not evil—it is natural—but it is the first narrowing of infinity."

His voice grew quieter.

"From comparison arises fear. Fear not because anything is wrong, but because something can now be *lost*. What was once boundless now appears bounded. What was eternal now imagines an end."

He looked at the seekers.

"And when fear arises, clinging follows. Clinging to form, to identity, to continuity. The Upanishad hints that the One, seeing this division, felt a subtle tremor—not pain, but vulnerability. The vulnerability of appearing as many."

Guruji nodded slowly.

"This clinging is the root of suffering. Not suffering imposed from outside, but suffering born from contraction. The infinite trying to hold itself in a finite shape."

He offered another image.

"Imagine a vast sky choosing to appear as a cloud. The cloud is beautiful, unique—but it fears dissolution. The sky never does. The suffering belongs to the cloud, not to the sky."

He let the silence breathe.

"This is why the sages did not call the world an error. They called it *lila*—a divine play. Suffering enters not because the play is cruel, but because the actor forgets he is acting."

Guruji said gently:

"The One never stopped being One.

Multiplicity did not break it.

But the moment the One forgot itself in its own reflection,
comparison arose,

fear followed,

clinging tightened,

and suffering appeared.

Not as a punishment—

but as the ache of infinity wearing a finite mask."

The hall was quiet. Not empty—full. As if the story had not been told, but *remembered* by everyone listening.

Guruji paused.

"This is echoed in the Buddhist teaching of *dependent origination*. The Buddha did not say suffering exists because the world is flawed. He said suffering arises because ignorance arises—ignorance of true nature. From ignorance comes identity, from identity desire, from desire attachment, and from attachment sorrow. The chain begins not with pain, but with misunderstanding."

Kiran frowned slightly. "So suffering is… a mistake?"

Guruji shook his head.

"No. That is where people go wrong. Suffering is not a cosmic error. It is a *local experience* of a universal truth."

He leaned forward.

"Think of the ocean. In its totality, it is vast, rhythmic, complete. But when the ocean appears as a wave, the wave is born with a beginning and a fear of ending. The wave suffers not because the ocean is cruel, but because the wave believes it is separate.

The ocean has no fear of death.

The wave does."

The Buddha Hall grew still, as if listening.

"This is why the Bhagavad Gita speaks of *avidya*—mistaken identity. Arjuna's suffering on the battlefield was not caused by the war alone, but by his narrowed identity: 'I am this body, this role, this doer.' Krishna does not remove the battlefield. He removes the illusion of separation."

Guruji's voice softened.

"When infinite wholeness is filtered through a limited lens—through a body, a name, a story—it feels like pressure. That pressure is experienced as pain, loss, longing, fear. Not because perfection has failed, but because perfection is being *experienced through limitation.*"

He looked at Kiran with compassion.

"Suffering is what perfection feels like when it forgets itself.

It is what eternity feels like when trapped in time.

What unity feels like when seen as separation.

What love feels like when mistaken for possession."

Kiran's eyes glistened. "Then… is suffering necessary?"

Guruji nodded slowly.

"Necessary—not as punishment, but as reminder. Pain is the friction created when the finite rubs against the infinite. It is the signal that something vast is trying to remember itself through you."

He placed the crystal back on the ground.

"When awareness widens, suffering does not instantly disappear—but it changes its meaning. Pain may still arise, but it is no longer personal. It becomes like thunder in the sky—loud, temporary, not owned."

He said gently:

"Perfection never broke.

Only perception narrowed.

And suffering is not reality's wound—

it is reality's whisper, urging the part to remember the whole."

Kiran bowed his head. The colours on the ground slowly faded as the sun shifted, but something inside him had quietly realigned—like a prism remembering it was once pure light.

Vidyarthi's question lingered in the hall like a bell struck softly but allowed to ring.

"Guruji," he asked, "are science and mysticism speaking of the same thing?"

Guruji did not answer immediately. He looked at the lamps lining the hall, then at the faces of the seekers, and finally at his own open palm—as though the answer rested there.

"Yes," he said at last, "but they speak in different languages, and they stand at different distances from the same fire."

He leaned forward slightly.

"Science approaches reality the way a careful cartographer approaches a vast land. It measures, maps, names, and classifies. It asks *how* things behave, under what laws, in what patterns. In doing so, it has revealed wonders—atoms that are mostly empty space, particles that behave like waves, time that bends, space that curves. Each discovery quietly dissolves the certainty of solidity."

A faint smile crossed his face.

"Mysticism, however, does not draw a map. It walks barefoot into the land. It does not ask *how* reality behaves, but *what it is* when all distance between knower and known collapses."

Guruji paused.

"In the *Upanishads*, the sages declared, *'Tat Tvam Asi'*—That Thou Art. This was not a philosophical claim, but a recognition arising in deep stillness. The knower dissolved into the known. No instruments were needed because the observer itself became the experiment."

He lifted a finger.

"Centuries later, science would discover something astonishing—that the observer affects the observed. In quantum physics, the act of measurement alters the outcome. The electron behaves differently depending on how it is watched."

He looked directly at Vidyarthi.

"Science stumbled upon what mystics had lived for millennia: separation is not absolute."

The hall felt closer, more intimate.

"In the *Tao Te Ching*, Laozi says, *'The Tao that can be spoken is not the eternal Tao.'* This is not a rejection of language, but an acknowledgment of its limits. Science speaks beautifully—but it must speak. Mysticism falls silent and lets reality speak through it."

Guruji offered another image.

"Imagine a man studying a river. Science measures its depth, speed, chemical composition, and source. All of this is true, valuable, and necessary. Mysticism enters the river, feels the current, is carried by it, and forgets the name 'river' altogether."

He paused.

"One approach gives power. The other gives belonging."

"In the *Kena Upanishad*, the gods believed their victory was their own achievement. Only when their power failed did they encounter the Absolute. Science, too, is powerful—and its power is real. But when it reaches the edge of explanation, when equations fall silent, humility opens the door to wonder."

Guruji's voice softened.

"Where science names, mysticism recognises.

Where science measures, mysticism remembers.

Where science stands outside and asks,

mysticism dissolves inside and knows."

He brought his hands together loosely.

"They are not enemies. Nor are they duplicates. They are two eyes of the same being—one analytical, one contemplative. With one eye, reality is impressive. With both, it becomes intimate."

He concluded:

"When science forgets mystery, it becomes arrogant.

When mysticism rejects reason, it becomes vague.

But when they walk together,

truth is not only understood—

it is lived."

The silence that followed was not empty. It was the silence of a question that had finally recognised itself in the answer.

CHAPTER III

God as Nature

"The universe is the only holy book written in action—every leaf a verse, every star a syllable of truth."

– Shree Shambav.

Synopsis

This chapter unveils nature not as a backdrop to spiritual life, but as its living body. Shree Shambav guides the seekers beyond the idea of God as an external ruler and reveals divinity as the very fabric of existence—breathing as forests, flowing as rivers, collapsing as stars, and healing as soil. The macrocosm of the universe mirrors itself perfectly within the microcosm of the human being; every cell carries the memory of galaxies, every breath echoes ancient rhythms. Ecology, in this vision, is no longer an ethical obligation enforced by fear or duty—it is awakened awareness. When unity is seen clearly, harm becomes incoherent, and care arises naturally. Reverence shifts from temples to trees, from scripture to seasons. Nature is not moralistic, yet it is profoundly intelligent—responding to alignment with harmony and to neglect with consequence. To live spiritually, Shree Shambav teaches, is to live ecologically, consciously, and intimately with the whole.

After the evening coffee break, the devotees returned to the Buddha Hall as one returns to a temple after a long pilgrimage—not outwardly exhausted, but inwardly rearranged. Their steps were lighter, slower, almost apologetic, as though the floor were no longer an object to be crossed but a presence to be honoured. The hum of casual conversation had dissolved somewhere between the cups of coffee and the corridors outside. What followed them back was not alertness, but attentiveness.

They sat.

They waited.

Not for instruction—but for attunement.

Guruji arrived without ceremony. No sound announced him. It felt, rather, as though the hall itself had been waiting for his form to complete its stillness. He took his seat gently, like a leaf settling on water, disturbing nothing yet changing everything. His gaze rested briefly on the horizon beyond the open hall, where the last gold of evening was surrendering to indigo. Dusk lingered there—neither day nor night—

like a truth suspended between knowing and becoming.

Minutes passed. Or perhaps time loosened its grip.

Then Guruji spoke.

“Have you noticed,” he said softly, “what ants do after the rain?”

Some of the devotees smiled faintly. Others frowned, unsure where the question was leading.

“Rain destroys their homes. Tunnels collapse. Order vanishes. And yet,” he continued, “no ant protests the sky. No ant curses the rain. They simply begin again. Grain by grain. Body by body.”

He paused.

“This,” he said, “is scripture.”

The words landed quietly, but deeply.

“In the ancient texts,” Guruji continued, “scripture was not always ink on palm leaves. The *Rishis* learned by watching rivers flow without resentment, trees shed leaves without grief, and stars burn themselves into extinction without complaint. Nature was their first teacher.”

He leaned forward slightly.

"God is not outside creation, supervising it like a ruler seated on a distant throne. God breathes as forests, collapses as stars, nourishes as soil, circulates as blood. God is not watching nature—God is *being* nature."

The hall felt suddenly vast, as though the walls had moved outward.

"In the *Taittirīya Upaniṣad*, it is said:

'From Bliss all beings are born, by Bliss they live, and into Bliss they return.'

Here, Bliss does not mean pleasure or emotional happiness. It signifies **Ānanda**—the self-existent, self-sustaining intelligence of life itself. It is the quiet rhythm that grows grass, heals wounds, and restores order after every storm."

Anandaaddhyeva khalvimāni bhutani jayante |

Anandena jatani jivanti |

Anandam prayantyabhisamvisantiti ||

Meaning:

From Bliss alone, indeed, all beings are born.

Born of Bliss, they live.

Into Bliss they move and finally merge.

Here **Ananda (Bliss)** does not refer to an emotional state. It points to **Brahman itself**—the self-caused, self-sustaining ground of all existence.

It is:

- the rhythm behind growth and decay
- the coherence beneath chaos
- the silent order that allows ants to rebuild, forests to heal, and stars to be born again

Guruji said, "This **Ananda** is the **God Frequency**—not an experience added to life, but the ground from which life continuously arises, lives, and returns."

Guruji gestured gently toward his chest.

"The universe is the macrocosm. You are the microcosm. What happens in galaxies happens in your cells. Stars are born, age, and die—and so do your thoughts. Nebulae swirl—and so does breath. Gravity binds planets—and longing binds hearts."

He let that settle.

"In the *Brihadaranyaka Upanishad*, the sage declares, *'As is the cosmos, so is the body; as is the body, so is the cosmos.'* This is not poetry—it is perception refined beyond division."

"Yatha pinde tatha brahmande"

He picked up a handful of soil from a small bowl near his seat.

“This feeds roots, which feed leaves, which feed air, which feeds lungs, which feed blood, which returns to soil. Tell me—where does God stop in this cycle?”

No one answered.

“Ecology,” Guruji said softly, “is not a moral obligation. It is not about being ‘good.’ It is recognition. When you harm the earth, you harm an extension of yourself. When you heal the soil, something in you breathes easier.”

He smiled gently.

“In the *Dhammapada*, the Buddha said, *‘The world is led by mind.’* But he did not mean human mind alone. He meant the intelligence that moves through all forms—ants rebuilding, trees leaning toward light, hearts learning compassion after loss.”

Guruji’s voice lowered.

“When you see God only in temples, you exploit forests.
When you see God only in heaven, you neglect the earth.

But when you see God as the ecosystem itself,

reverence becomes natural.”

He said, almost in a whisper:

"The ants do not pray.

They participate.

And in their participation,

the divine is already complete."

Silence returned—not as absence, but as agreement.

Aastha's question lingered in the hall like a bell whose echo had not yet decided where to rest.

"Guruji," she asked softly, "how does ecological harm affect consciousness?"

Guruji reached down, gathered a small pinch of soil from the earthen bowl beside him, and let it fall slowly back into the bowl. The grains made no sound. Still, everyone felt the gesture.

"Aastha," he said gently, "ecological harm is not only environmental—it is perceptual."

He lifted his gaze, letting it travel across the hall, across the unseen forests, rivers, and mountains beyond its walls.

"When we wound the Earth, we rehearse separation. When we poison waters, we practice forgetting. When forests fall, something collapses silently inside the human psyche as well."

He paused.

"The outer world and the inner world are not two. They only appear so to a divided mind."

The Ancient Mirror

"In the *Atharva Veda*," Guruji continued, "the Earth is addressed as *Bhumi Mata*—Mother Earth. Not as poetry, but as recognition. A mother is not merely a provider; she is the environment in which consciousness first learns safety, trust, and belonging. When a child grows in neglect, the wound does not stay in the body alone—it shapes perception, fear, and identity."

He leaned forward slightly.

"Humanity is now a child harming its own mother. And the anxiety you see spreading across minds, nations, and generations is not accidental. It is ecological trauma translated into psychological unrest."

The Story of the Ashram Well

"Let me tell you a story," Guruji said.

"There was once an ashram that drew water from a single well. For years, the monks used it with reverence. They drew only what was needed. They cleaned its edges. They sat beside it in silence.

Over time, new residents arrived—clever, efficient, hurried. They dug deeper channels to extract more water, faster. 'The well is strong,' they said. 'It has always given.'"

Guruji's voice softened.

"Soon, the water turned bitter. Illness spread. The monks argued—some blamed bad karma, others blamed fate. Only one old woman said, 'We did not poison the water. We poisoned our relationship with it.'"

The hall was utterly still.

"When the well was healed—rested, cleaned, respected—the water cleared. And so did the people."

Fragmented Land, Fragmented Mind

"Consciousness," Guruji said, "is not sealed inside the skull. It breathes with landscapes. A mind raised among concrete, noise, and exploitation struggles to settle—not because it is weak, but because its environment is restless."

He gestured outward.

"When rivers are dammed violently, human emotions become dammed. When forests are erased, imagination thins. When soil is stripped of life, patience disappears from society. This is not coincidence. It is correspondence."

"In the *Taittiriya Upanishad*, it is said that beings arise from *Ananda*—a sustaining harmony. When that harmony is violated externally, inner ananda contracts into anxiety, craving, and fear."

Healing Is One Movement

"Do not imagine," Guruji said firmly, "that meditation alone will heal a world that lives in ecological violence. And do not imagine that environmental reform alone will succeed without inner transformation."

He smiled softly.

"Healing nature and healing consciousness are not parallel tasks. They are the same movement, seen at different distances."

"To plant a tree with awareness is meditation. To drink water with reverence is prayer. To walk gently upon the Earth is philosophy enacted."

“When you stand barefoot on soil,” Guruji said, “your nervous system listens. When you look at the sky without ownership, the mind remembers its scale. When you protect a river, something ancient in you exhales.”

He let the silence speak.

“A poisoned land breeds poisoned awareness. A healed Earth invites a healed humanity. The Earth does not need saving from us—we need remembering through her.”

Aastha lowered her eyes, not in sorrow, but in recognition.

Abhirami’s voice rose gently from the stillness, carrying neither challenge nor doubt—only sincerity.

“Guruji,” she asked, “can reverence replace religion?”

Guruji spoke, slowly, as one tracing a river back to its source.

“Abhirami,” he said, “reverence is not a substitute for religion; it is its fulfilment.”

Before Temples, There Was Awe

"Before the first temple was built," Guruji continued, "before the first mantra was memorised, before the first scripture was bound, there was awe."

He gestured toward the open sky beyond the hall.

"When early humans saw lightning tear the heavens, when they watched seeds disappear into soil and return as food, when they witnessed birth and death, they did not call it 'religion.' They stood silent. That silence was reverence."

"In the *Rig Veda*, the sages do not begin with commandments. They begin with wonder: *'Who truly knows? Who can say how creation arose?'* That question itself is reverence."

The Story of the Unnamed Shrine

"Let me tell you a story," Guruji said.

"There was once a village with no temple. At its edge stood an ancient tree. People rested beneath it, wept beneath it, celebrated beneath it. No idol was carved. No priest was appointed."

"Years later, a grand temple was built elsewhere, and the tree was forgotten. Rituals became elaborate. Arguments arose about correctness. Yet peace did not increase."

"One day, during a drought, the villagers gathered again beneath the old tree. No chants were spoken. No rules followed. They sat in silence, listening to the wind."

Guruji smiled softly.

"That evening, rain came."

"Not because the tree was holier than the temple," he added gently, "but because reverence had returned."

Religion as Structure, Reverence as Life

"Religion organizes belief," Guruji said. "It creates maps, methods, memory. This is not wrong. But maps are not the land."

"When belief hardens without reverence, religion becomes habit. When reverence disappears, rituals become empty gestures—performed by the body, not inhabited by the soul."

"In the *Bhagavad Gita*, Krishna does not say, 'Believe in me.' He says, *'See me in all beings.'* That seeing is reverence."

Reverence Dissolves Distance

"Reverence dissolves the distance between sacred and ordinary," Guruji continued.

"When reverence awakens, walking becomes worship. Eating becomes communion. Listening becomes scripture."

"A person who bows inwardly to life does not need commandments to act kindly. Compassion arises naturally, the way fragrance arises from a flower."

"In Zen, there is a saying: *'Chop wood, carry water.'* Not as instruction—but as revelation. When reverence is present, nothing is mundane."

The Living Scripture

Guruji's voice softened further.

"Religion often asks you to look upward. Reverence teaches you to look inward—and outward at the same time."

"To the leaf. To the ant. To the stranger. To your own breath."

"When you truly revere life, dogma loosens its grip. Fear gives way to care. Control yields to intimacy."

He paused, allowing the hall to breathe.

"Religion may guide you to the door," he said, "but reverence is what allows you to live inside the sacred."

Abhirami's eyes glistened—not with answers, but with recognition.

Kieron's question emerged slowly, as though it had been waiting for the right stillness to speak.

"Guruji," he asked, "is nature moral or neutral?"

Guruji closed his eyes for a brief moment, not to withdraw, but to listen—perhaps to the wind outside, perhaps to something far older. When he opened them, his gaze was clear and steady.

"Kieron," he said softly, "nature is neither moral nor indifferent—it is intelligent."

Beyond Punishment and Reward

"It does not punish, and it does not forgive," Guruji continued. "Those ideas belong to the human mind, shaped by law, society, and fear. Nature does not sit in judgment. It responds."

He lifted his hand slightly, as if weighing something invisible.

"When you place your hand in fire, the fire does not punish you. It burns. Not out of cruelty, but out of consistency. Fire is loyal to its nature."

"So too with rivers, forests, climates, and bodies. Harmony invites nourishment. Imbalance invites correction."

"In the *Ṛta* of the Vedas," Guruji said, "the universe is described as an ordered intelligence—a cosmic rhythm. The sun rises not because it is commanded, but because it belongs to this order. Seasons change not as reward or punishment, but as response to alignment."

He paused.

"When humans live within Ṛta, life feels supported. When we violate it, life feels harsh—not because it has turned against us, but because we have turned against its rhythm."

The Story of the Flooded City

"Let me tell you a story," Guruji said.

"There was once a city built beside a river. The river was honoured at first—its floodplains left open, its cycles respected. The city prospered."

"Later, embankments were raised, wetlands filled, forests upstream cut. The people said, 'We have mastered the river.'"

Guruji's voice grew quiet.

"When the flood came, it was called a disaster. But the river had not changed its nature. It had only responded."

"Was the flood immoral?" he asked gently. "Or was it intelligent correction?"

Resonance, Not Judgment

"Nature operates through resonance," Guruji said. "It amplifies what we align with."

"Care invites regeneration. Exploitation invites collapse. Stillness invites clarity. Violence invites turbulence."

"In Taoism, this is called the *Dao*—the way things move when not resisted. Water flows around obstacles, but it wears down what blocks it."

Human Morality and Natural Intelligence

"Morality is a human language," Guruji said, "created to guide behaviour in society. Nature does not speak this language—but it speaks a deeper one."

"It speaks in feedback."

"When forests vanish, climates shift. When soil dies, food weakens. When noise fills the world, minds lose silence."

"These are not punishments. They are messages."

The Teaching Hidden in Response

"When we align," Guruji said, "life feels generous. When we resist, life feels instructive."

"Nature is not cruel. It is precise."

"It does not hate us. It mirrors us."

The hall remained silent, not heavy, but awake—like land after rain, listening carefully to what it had always been saying.

Guruji rose from his asana without ceremony.

There was no closing mantra, no final instruction. His leaving itself was the teaching.

He bowed—not to the people, but to the silence that had ripened through the day—and walked out of the Buddha Hall. The session was complete, not because words had ended, but because something essential had settled.

One by one, the devotees followed. Footsteps faded. Cushions lay undisturbed. The hall emptied of bodies, yet it was far from empty.

The Buddha Hall retained a warmth, as though the air itself remembered how it had been listened to. The night had fully arrived. Above, the sky stretched wide and clear, stars scattered like quiet witnesses. Clouds drifted slowly, playing hide and seek with constellations older than human naming. Wind moved through the courtyards, not aimlessly, but with the intimacy of one who knows every corner of the place.

Frogs croaked their nocturnal hymns near the water. Insects hummed in layered rhythms. Somewhere in the distance, a night bird called out—long, haunting, unafraid of silence. The world had not gone to sleep. It had simply changed teachers.

The devotees walked toward the food centre, hunger now gentle, unhurried. Dinner was simple, nourishing. No one rushed. Even eating felt quieter, more deliberate, as though the body itself was listening to the day's teachings.

After the meal, a small group lingered.

Vidyarthi, Aastha, Akshaya, Kiran, Padma, Vasudeva, and Abhirami gathered near the old fireplace. Someone had already lit it. Flames rose and fell, licking the cool night air, casting living shadows across their faces. Fire cracked softly, speaking in its ancient language. The warmth drew them inward—not just toward the flame, but toward one another.

Conversation flowed without effort.

They spoke of small moments from the day—a sentence that stayed, a silence that lingered longer than expected. Laughter surfaced too, light and human, dissolving the weight of abstraction. Guruji's words returned again and again, not quoted, but lived through reflection.

Gradually, others arrived.

Bhavya and Aarna came first, still carrying the calm of an evening walk. Dev, Sam, Alice, Sofia, and John followed, their presence easy, their smiles unforced. Nita, Lalitha, Rohith, and Sujitha joined soon after, bringing tea and quiet cheer.

The circle widened naturally, like ripples finding one another.

Akshatha arrived with Apeksha, Abhilasha, Akanksh, and Roopa, their faces thoughtful, eyes still inward-turned. Then Aurora, Ginevra, Emma, Giorgia, Greta, Martina, and Beatrice appeared, followed by Kieron, Astyn, Espen, Greta, and Divyani. No one announced themselves. They simply took their place around the fire.

For a while, there was only the sound of burning wood and night insects.

Then Greta's voice rose—calm, expectant, carrying a gentle authority earned through listening.

"Apeksha," she said softly, "it's time for your story… to complete the day."

Smiles moved through the circle like a shared breath.

All eyes turned.

Apeksha did not begin immediately. She stared into the fire, watching embers collapse into ash, sparks rise and vanish. When she spoke, her voice was steady, but tender.

"There is a story," she said, "that my grandmother once told me when I was a child."

"There was a village at the edge of a forest. The villagers believed the forest was sacred, but over time, they stopped visiting it. Life became busy. Rituals replaced relationship. Prayers were said inside walls, not beneath trees."

"One year, a long drought came. Crops failed. Wells dried. The villagers prayed harder, argued louder, blamed fate and gods."

"One evening, a small child wandered into the forest alone. He was not searching for water or answers—only silence. He sat beneath an old tree and listened."

Apeksha paused. Firelight danced across her face.

"The wind moved. Leaves rustled. The child felt no miracle, heard no voice. Yet something softened inside him. He placed his palms on the earth and rested."

"When he returned to the village, he said only one thing: 'The forest is still breathing.'"

The group leaned in.

"The elders laughed at first. But something in the child's stillness unsettled them. The next day, a few followed him back—not to ask, not to demand, but to sit."

"They cleared nothing. They took nothing. They listened."

"Over weeks, clouds returned. Not suddenly. Slowly. Soil softened. Seeds sprouted. The forest did not reward them—it responded."

Apeksha looked around the circle.

"The drought did not end because prayers were answered. It ended because relationship was restored."

She lowered her gaze.

"My grandmother said: *When humans remember how to belong, the Earth remembers how to nourish.*"

Silence followed—not empty, but full.

The fire crackled, collapsing inward, glowing deeper as its flames softened. Above them, stars watched patiently. No one hurried to speak. There was nothing to add.

One by one, the devotees rose. Goodnights were exchanged quietly. Footsteps drifted away into different paths leading to their chambers.

The fire was left to burn down on its own.

Embers glowed softly, holding the memory of heat without flame—just as each heart carried the day's teachings without words.

That night, Kanchipuram was not merely wrapped in darkness.

It became a sanctuary.

A bridge between what had been understood and what was yet to be lived.

A reminder that even in stillness, learning continues—quietly, faithfully—like stars that do not speak, yet never stop guiding.

PART TWO

GOD FREQUENCY

"Long before life asked questions, the universe was already answering with form."

- *Shree Shambav*

CHAPTER IV

The Infinite Frequency

"Fear is not darkness; it is incoherent rhythm mistaken for truth."

– Shree Shambav.

Synopsis

This chapter explores reality as vibration rather than structure, revealing consciousness as a field of frequencies continuously seeking coherence. Guruji introduces stillness as the highest resonance—not absence, but perfect alignment—where awareness restores harmony without force. Emotions are reframed as vibrational states: fear as fragmentation, love as coherence, pain as distorted signal. Drawing from ancient wisdom and modern insight, the chapter dissolves the divide between spirituality and science, presenting meditation not as escape but as recalibration. Society itself is examined as a collective instrument capable of harmony or noise depending on its inner tuning. Through story, silence, and subtle teaching, the reader is guided to recognise that peace is not attained through effort but remembered through alignment. The chapter invites a shift from controlling life to listening to it—where healing, clarity, and meaning arise naturally when frequency returns to its original song.

The words settled into the hall like a stone dropped into still water.

For a moment, no one moved.

Somewhere beyond the walls of Buddha Hall, a distant temple drum sounded—irregular, uneven. Its rhythm faltered, paused, resumed. It was not part of any ritual. It was simply a sound arising in the morning air.

Guruji's gaze softened, as though he were listening not to the drum itself, but to what it revealed.

Guruji said softly, "Let me share a story."

He paused, as though allowing the story to arrive before the words.

"Once, a young seeker came to his teacher, burdened by an invisible storm. His eyes carried devotion, but his voice trembled with exhaustion. He bowed and said,
'Master, my mind does not rest. I meditate, I chant, I serve others—yet within me there is only noise. Every effort feels sincere, yet peace does not stay.'

"The teacher listened without interruption. He did not offer counsel, nor did he correct the boy's practice. After a long silence, he simply gestured for the seeker to follow.

"They walked until they reached a river.

"The teacher asked the boy to sit beside it."

Guruji's eyes moved slowly across the faces before him, ensuring no word was rushed.

"At first, the river roared. Stones collided, branches scraped, currents fought. The boy covered his ears. But the teacher said, 'Wait.' Hours passed. The sun climbed. The river did not change—but the boy did. Slowly, the noise revealed a rhythm. Beneath the chaos, there was order. Beneath the force, there was flow.

"The teacher then asked, 'Did the river become calm, or did your listening mature?'"

Guruji paused.

"When fear governs life," he said, "we hear only collision. Thoughts crash into one another. Desires compete. Memories interrupt the present. The rhythm of existence becomes uneven—not because life is broken, but because listening is fractured."

Aastha felt her breath tighten—not from anxiety, but recognition. Akshaya lowered his eyes, sensing the quiet truth beneath the words.

"In the *Mahabharata*," Guruji continued, "Arjuna stands between two armies. The battlefield is not merely outside—it is inside him. His breath is uneven. His bow trembles. Krishna does not accuse him. He simply says, *'You are hearing life through fear.'* That is why the Gita begins not with action, but with clarity of perception."

The oil lamps flickered, as if affirming the teaching.

"Fear does not shout," Guruji said softly. "It distorts rhythm. It makes the drumbeat erratic. One moment too fast, another too slow. One day grasping, the next retreating. This is how fear lives—not as terror, but as inconsistency."

He leaned forward slightly.

"But when reverence replaces fear," he said, "life regains its cadence. Breath aligns. Action flows. Even pain finds timing. Even silence has meaning."

Outside, the temple drum sounded again—this time steadier, as though the drummer himself had settled.

Guruji smiled faintly.

"Do not fight the sound of your life," he said. "Listen deeper. Beneath every uneven beat is an intelligence waiting for trust. When fear loosens its grip, existence begins to play you—not as noise, but as music."

No one spoke.

No one needed to.

The morning light grew stronger, spilling gently through the hall, touching faces, lamps, and folded hands alike. And in that quiet illumination, many realised something subtle yet profound: the drumbeat they had feared was not an enemy—it was an invitation to learn how to listen.

Guruji's voice did not rise; it settled—like dust falling back to the earth after a storm.

He said,

"God is frequency, not form.

Stillness is the highest resonance.

Pain, love, fear—each vibrates.

Awareness restores harmony."

He paused, letting the words find their own place inside the listeners.

"Human thought longs to *see* God," he continued, "to name Him, to give Him edges and a face. But the ancient seers listened instead. They did not ask, *What does God look like?* They asked, *What does reality sound like when nothing is disturbed?*"

He gestured gently, as if touching the air.

"In the **Rig Veda**, creation begins not with an image but with a vibration—*Nada*. Before form, before light, before matter, there was resonance. Even modern science arrives here at last: atoms are not solid things; they are oscillations. What you call matter is music slowed down."

The hall felt as though it were breathing.

"In the **Mandukya Upanishad**, Brahman is described through *Om*—not as a symbol, but as a frequency that contains waking, dreaming, deep sleep, and that which transcends them. Om is not pronounced to reach God. Om is pronounced to remember the frequency you already are."

He leaned forward slightly.

"Stillness," Guruji said, "is not absence of movement. It is perfect coherence. When all vibrations align, no friction is felt. This is why sages sit in silence. Silence is not empty—it is tuned."

He smiled faintly.

"Chaos is not evil. Chaos is fragmented resonance. Like an orchestra where each instrument plays sincerely, but without listening to the whole."

He allowed the metaphor to settle, then continued.

"Pain has a frequency.

Love has a frequency.

Fear has a frequency."

"In the **Bhagavad Gita**, Krishna tells Arjuna that fear arises when one forgets their own nature. Fear is not a sin—it is a low coherence state, a mind vibrating against itself. That is why fear exhausts you. It is not heavy—it is *noisy.*"

He lifted a finger gently, as if tuning an unseen string.

"Love, on the other hand, is high coherence. When you love, your breath slows, your muscles soften, your thoughts synchronise. Love does not add energy—it removes resistance."

He paused.

"And pain," he said quietly, "is not punishment. Pain is a distorted signal. Like a drum struck too tightly, its sound becomes sharp and unbearable. The problem is not the drum. It is the tension."

The listeners felt something loosen inside their chests.

"In the **Buddha's teaching**, suffering arises not from sensation, but from *tanha*—clinging. Clinging forces life into a narrow frequency band. Awareness widens the band. And when awareness widens, harmony returns."

He looked around the hall, meeting no one in particular and everyone at once.

"Awareness does not fight fear.

Awareness does not suppress pain.

Awareness listens."

"And in listening," Guruji said, "the frequency naturally retunes itself."

He closed his eyes briefly.

"This is why healing is not about fixing what is broken. It is about restoring resonance."

A long silence followed—dense, alive, unmistakably present.

Then Guruji added softly,

"God is not found by climbing upward. God is remembered when the noise falls away."

And in that stillness, something within each listener recognised its original sound—not as a thought, not as a belief, but as a quiet, unwavering hum that had always been there.

Rohith's question did not rise from curiosity alone; it carried the quiet weight of lived experience. His voice held the unspoken confession of nights where the mind raced ahead of the heart, and mornings where emotions arrived before meaning. When he asked, *"Guruji, how do emotions alter frequency?"* the hall listened differently—as though the question belonged to everyone.

"Emotions," Guruji began softly, "are not visitors in consciousness. They are movements of consciousness."

He looked around the hall.

"When awareness flows freely, emotion becomes music. When awareness tightens, emotion becomes noise."

The Inner Instrument

"Consider a veena," Guruji said, invoking an image familiar to all. "The same string can produce divine melody or unbearable sound. The difference is not the string—it is the tension."

He paused.

"Fear tightens the string of awareness. Love loosens it into resonance."

Fear, he explained, does not merely frighten the mind—it contracts perception itself. Breath shortens. Muscles brace. Thought narrows. The world feels hostile not because it is, but because awareness has folded inward to defend itself. In that contraction, frequency fragments. Life feels sharp, rushed, dissonant.

Love does the opposite.

"When love enters," Guruji said, "the string relaxes. Breath deepens. Vision widens. You feel connected—not because something new has arrived, but because nothing is being resisted."

Guruji then turned toward ancient memory.

"In the *Chandogya Upanishad*," he said, "there is the teaching *Tat Tvam Asi—That Thou Art*. But notice this: when the student hears it in fear, it sounds like philosophy. When he hears it in love, it becomes recognition."

The truth does not change. The **frequency of the listener** does.

"In fear," Guruji continued, "even truth feels threatening. In love, even uncertainty feels safe."

A Story of the Lake

"Let me tell you a story," Guruji said.

"There was once a king who came to a sage, troubled by visions. 'When I look at the world,' he said, 'I see enemies everywhere.' The sage led him to a lake at dusk. The water was restless from wind. The king saw only broken reflections—trees twisted, moon shattered."

"The sage said nothing. He simply waited."

"As night deepened, the wind fell silent. The water stilled. The same lake now reflected the moon perfectly."

Guruji looked at Rohith.

"The moon did not move. The lake did."

Emotion as Frequency, Not Fault

"Understand this," Guruji said gently. "An emotion is never a mistake. It is information about your inner tuning."

Anger signals compressed energy seeking release. Grief signals love searching for continuity. Fear signals attention trapped in separation.

“When you resist emotion,” he said, “you trap its frequency. When you witness it, the frequency completes its movement.”

This is why ancient traditions emphasised *sakshi bhava*—the stance of the witness. Not to suppress emotion, not to indulge it, but to **see** it.

“In the *Bhagavad Gita*,” Guruji reminded them, “Krishna does not ask Arjuna to destroy emotion. He asks him to stand steady within it.”

Vibrational Literacy

“Modern people try to manage emotions,” Guruji said softly. “Ancient wisdom taught how to **listen** to them.”

He smiled.

“To be emotionally aware is not to be emotionally overwhelmed. It is to become musically sensitive—to know when the note is sharp, when it is flat, and how to retune without breaking the string.”

When emotions are met with awareness, their frequency naturally recalibrates. Fear softens into alertness. Anger clarifies into strength. Grief matures into compassion.

"Then," Guruji said, "emotion no longer rules consciousness. It serves it."

He looked at Rohith with warmth.

"This is vibrational literacy—the ability to read the music of your inner life, and to return again and again to harmony."

The hall was silent—not empty, but tuned.

Sujitha's question did not sound theoretical. It carried the ache of someone who had watched the world grow louder but not wiser, faster but not kinder. When she asked, *"Guruji, can society be tuned like an instrument?"* her voice held both doubt and longing—the doubt born of history, and the longing born of hope.

Guruji looked at her for a long moment, as one listens before responding to a complex raga.

"Yes," he said gently, "but not the way machines are tuned."

The Orchestra of Many Lives

"A society," Guruji continued, "is not a single instrument. It is an orchestra of different temperaments, histories, wounds, and gifts. Harmony does not arise when every instrument plays the same note—it arises when each listens to the whole."

He paused.

"When listening disappears, even skilled musicians create noise."

Fear, he explained, is the greatest disrupter of collective rhythm. When fear dominates a society—fear of loss, of the other, of scarcity—institutions begin to vibrate at that frequency. Laws harden. Economies compete rather than cooperate. Media amplifies outrage. The result is not order, but chronic dissonance disguised as strength.

Guruji's voice deepened as he turned toward ancient memory.

"In the *Mahabharata*," he said, "the Kaurava court was not lacking intelligence, power, or advisors. It lacked *listening*. Each voice sought dominance, not harmony."

Bhishma knew what was right. Vidura spoke wisdom. Drona foresaw disaster. Yet fear—of losing power, of appearing weak—kept the court out of tune. The war did not arise because society lacked knowledge. It arose because it lacked coherence.

"Knowledge without attunement," Guruji said, "becomes weaponry."

The Buddha's Bell

He then offered another image.

"In Buddhist monasteries," Guruji said, "there is a practice of ringing a bell. When the bell is struck, all activity pauses. Everyone listens until the sound dissolves into silence."

He smiled softly.

"That bell is not for sound. It is for **alignment**."

A society, he explained, needs such bells—not always literal, but symbolic: moments of collective pause, reflection, remembrance of shared humanity. Without them, speed replaces wisdom, and progress loses direction.

Why Control Fails and Alignment Works

"Societies fail," Guruji said, "when they attempt to tune through force."

Control tightens the strings. Surveillance sharpens fear. Punishment increases resistance. The sound becomes shrill.

"Alignment," he continued, "loosens tension without breaking structure."

Education that teaches children how to listen inwardly before reacting outwardly. Leadership that models accountability rather than dominance. Economies that honour sufficiency instead of endless hunger. Cultures that measure success not only by growth, but by well-being.

“In the *Tao Te Ching*,” Guruji added, “it is said: *When the leader is silent, the people are aligned.* This is not passivity—it is resonance.”

The Smallest Tuning Fork

Sujitha listened closely as Guruji leaned forward slightly.

“Never forget,” he said, “a single tuned instrument can retune a room.”

Societies do not shift first through revolutions of policy, but through revolutions of perception. When individuals live with coherence—where thought, speech, and action resonate—others unconsciously entrain to that frequency.

“This is why saints unsettled empires,” Guruji said softly. “They did not argue. They resonated.”

The Deeper Answer

“So yes,” Guruji said, looking at Sujitha, “society can be tuned—but only by those willing to listen before they speak, feel before they judge, and align before they act."

He smiled.

"A society in harmony is not quiet. It is musical."

The hall remained still, but something subtle had shifted—like instruments gently adjusting themselves, one by one, to a deeper, shared note.

Astyn's question rose quietly, yet it carried the weight of a modern confusion shared by many. His voice was steady, but beneath it lay an unspoken doubt—the doubt of one who had seen meditation used as hiding, as spiritual bypass, as a polite withdrawal from the rough edges of life.

"Guruji," he asked, "is meditation alignment or escape?"

Guruji did not answer at once. He closed his eyes, as if listening to the question from beneath its words. When he spoke, his voice was calm, unhurried, and precise—like a river that knows its course.

"Meditation is often mistaken for withdrawal," he said. "But its true nature is **return**."

Returning, Not Running Away

"Escape," Guruji continued, "moves away from life. Meditation moves **into** it—without distortion."

He explained that escapism seeks numbness: silence to avoid pain, solitude to avoid responsibility, stillness to avoid engagement. Meditation, by contrast, sharpens perception. It removes the noise that prevents us from seeing clearly.

"When the inner waters are turbulent," Guruji said, "even the moon appears broken. Meditation does not remove the moon—it stills the water."

Arjuna's Pause on the Battlefield

Guruji turned gently toward an ancient memory.

"In the *Bhagavad Gita*," he said, "Arjuna does not flee the battlefield to meditate. He collapses *within* it."

Surrounded by chaos, grief, and moral confusion, Arjuna pauses—not to escape war, but to see clearly within it. Krishna does not tell him to renounce action. He teaches him **alignment**—how to act without fragmentation, how to stand in stillness while life demands movement.

"That pause," Guruji said, "was meditation."

Not a retreat from reality, but a recalibration before engagement.

The Bow and the String

Guruji lifted his hand, shaping an invisible bow.

"A bowstring," he said, "must be tightened to the right tension. Too loose, and the arrow falls. Too tight, and it snaps."

"Meditation is the act of tuning the string."

It restores the natural tension between effort and surrender, thought and awareness, action and rest. From that tuning, life can be lived with precision rather than reactivity.

Witnessing Without Fragmentation

He continued, "True meditation does not silence thoughts by force. It witnesses them until they lose their authority."

In the *Yoga Sutras*, Patanjali does not say *destroy the mind.* He says *still the fluctuations.* When waves settle, the lake does not disappear—it reflects reality as it is.

"Escapism avoids the waves," Guruji said. "Meditation learns how to float."

The Cup That Could Not Receive

"There was once a learned visitor who travelled a great distance to meet a Monk renowned for his insight. The visitor carried with him many books, many questions, and even more conclusions. His words arrived before his breath had settled. Before the monk could respond, the visitor explained his philosophy, his practices, his understanding of truth—each sentence an attempt to impress, to confirm, to be affirmed.

The monk listened without interruption. His face was calm, his eyes clear. When the visitor finally paused, expecting an answer, the monk rose silently and went to prepare tea.

They sat facing one another.

The monk poured tea into the visitor's cup. The liquid rose to the brim—and then continued. Tea spilled over the edges, ran across the table, and dripped onto the floor.

Startled, the visitor exclaimed, 'Master! The cup is full. Can't you see? No more will go in!'

The monk set the teapot down gently and said, 'Just so.'

He looked at the visitor with neither judgment nor irony, only clarity.

'You come to me like this cup—already full of opinions, beliefs, and borrowed wisdom. How can I offer you tea when there is no space to receive it? First empty the cup. Then we can speak.'"

Guruji paused, letting the image settle.

"This," he said quietly, "is the difference between information and transformation."

He explained that the monk was not dismissing knowledge. He was pointing to its limit. A mind crowded with conclusions cannot encounter truth freshly. Even the highest teachings become noise when the listener is already speaking inwardly.

"Emptiness," Guruji continued, "is not ignorance. It is availability."

In ancient texts, this is called *shunyata*—not a void, but openness. Like fertile soil that appears empty yet can receive rain, seed, and sun.

"A full cup reflects nothing," Guruji said. "An empty cup can hold the sky."

He leaned forward slightly.

"Meditation is the act of emptying—not by force, but by seeing. When thoughts are seen clearly, they loosen their grip. When identity softens, space appears. In that space, truth does not need to be explained. It reveals itself."

The hall remained still.

Somewhere inside, a few cups quietly tipped—making room.

"Meditation," Guruji smiled, "is that emptying—not of life, but of excess noise."

Astyn listened as Guruji's voice softened.

"When meditation is alignment, it makes you more available—to suffering, to responsibility, to love. When it is escape, it makes you distant, numb, spiritually polite but inwardly absent."

He paused.

"You will know the difference by its fruit. Escape makes you smaller. Alignment makes you spacious."

Guruji looked around the hall.

"Meditation is not a refuge from chaos," he said. "It is the art of moving through chaos without losing coherence."

Silence followed—not empty silence, but aligned silence. And in that stillness, many felt something subtle but unmistakable: not the urge to withdraw from life, but the quiet readiness to meet it fully, clearly, and whole.

CHAPTER V

Attributes and the Limits of Knowing

"Truth is larger than the window you stand at."

– Shree Shambav.

Synopsis

This chapter reveals reality as a single substance with infinite attributes, while acknowledging the profound limitation of human perception. Shree Shambav teaches that human beings can access only two attributes—thought and extension—mind and matter—yet mistakenly treat these partial views as total truth. From this misunderstanding arise spiritual conflict, dogma, and division. Through story, silence, and insight, Guruji reframes ignorance not as failure but as a sacred boundary that invites humility. Science and spirituality are presented not as opposites, but as complementary approaches—two windows of the same house—each incomplete alone, yet powerful together. The chapter calls for epistemic humility: a way of knowing that honors reason without denying mystery. In doing so, it dissolves the false war between faith and intellect, inviting a deeper unity where inquiry remains open, reverence remains alive, and truth is approached without violence.

The Buddha Hall rested in a luminous hush. Afternoon light spilled through the tall windows and settled gently on the stone floor, illuminating drifting dust motes that floated like unclaimed thoughts—present, unhurried, waiting. After the midday meal and a brief, restorative rest, the devotees returned as one returns to a river after crossing a long stretch of land: slower, quieter, inwardly attuned. The hall did not fill with movement or sound; it filled with readiness.

Guruji entered without ceremony and took his asana. He did not speak at once. His stillness itself seemed to listen—to the breath of the room, to the unspoken questions lingering from the morning. Silence gathered naturally, like birds settling at dusk.

When he finally spoke, his voice carried a gravity that did not press downward but drew the heart inward.

"This," he said softly, "is the moment many traditions gesture toward—but few pause long enough to see."

He let the words rest, as if allowing them to find their own place.

Then Guruji said, "A blind man once touched fire and cried, 'It is pain.'"

He paused, his gaze gentle, unwavering.

"He was not wrong," Guruji continued. "But he touched only one attribute."

The Blind Touching the Infinite

Guruji explained that this story appears in many forms across wisdom traditions. In Buddhist teachings, the blind men and the elephant touch different parts and argue over truth. In Sufi lore, seekers describe the same flame as destruction, warmth, or light depending on distance. In the Bible, Moses encounters God as fire in the burning bush—fire that burns yet does not consume. Each encounter is true, yet none is complete.

"God," Guruji said, "has infinite attributes."

The hall felt as though it leaned closer.

"But human perception is limited. We are given only two windows."

He raised one finger.

"Thought—mind, memory, interpretation, identity. The world as understood."

He raised another.

"Extension—form, matter, space, touch. The world as experienced."

"These two are not errors," he said. "They are gifts. But conflict begins when a part declares itself the whole."

When Parts Pretend to Be Totality

Guruji spoke of how suffering arises not from ignorance, but from certainty. When thought claims supremacy, reality becomes an argument. When extension alone is trusted, life becomes mechanical. Wars, dogmas, and divisions are born when partial vision demands absolute obedience.

"In the Bible," Guruji said, "Paul writes, 'Now we see through a glass, darkly.' Not falsely—dimly. The tragedy is not that the glass exists, but that we forget it is glass."

In Sufi poetry, Rumi warns, *'You have been taught how to speak, but not how to listen.'* Listening, Guruji said, is the surrender of partial knowing.

Two Windows, One House

Guruji's voice softened.

"Science and spirituality are not enemies. They are two windows of the same house. One looks outward, measuring extension. The other looks inward, exploring thought. Neither can see the whole sky alone."

He gestured subtly to the hall.

"When science denies mystery, it becomes arrogant. When spirituality denies matter, it becomes ungrounded. Truth requires both humility and wholeness."

The devotees sat quietly, many sensing something loosen within themselves—the need to defend one side, one belief, one language.

Guruji said gently:

"Conflict does not arise because humans see too little. It arises because we believe what we see is all there is."

Silence returned—not as absence, but as spacious understanding.

In that silence, thought rested. Extension softened. And for a fleeting moment, the house felt whole again.

Alice asked, "Guruji, how do we honor what we cannot know?"

Guruji listened to Alice with a softness that suggested the question itself was already a form of prayer.

He did not answer immediately.

Instead, he closed his eyes for a moment, as if turning inward to consult something older than language. When he spoke, his voice was gentle, but it carried the weight of lived truth.

Honouring the Unknowable

"Alice," Guruji said, "to honour what we cannot know is to bow without trying to own."

He looked around the hall, then lifted his hand slightly, as though holding something invisible.

"The mind is trained to conquer—to name, define, and conclude. But the deepest truths are not conquered. They are encountered."

He paused.

"When mystery is reduced to belief, it shrinks. When it is allowed to remain mystery, it expands us."

Guruji continued, "In the *Brihadaranyaka Upanishad*, Yajnavalkya is questioned again and again about the ultimate reality. Each time, he answers not with explanation, but with negation—*neti, neti*—not this, not that."

He smiled faintly.

"He was not being evasive. He was protecting truth from imprisonment. By refusing to define the Absolute, he preserved its vastness."

Guruji leaned forward slightly.

"To say *neti, neti* is not ignorance—it is reverence."

A Reflection from the Bible

"In the *Book of Job*," Guruji said, his voice steady and measured, "there is a man described as righteous—faithful, generous, blameless in his conduct. And yet, suffering falls upon him without warning."

He paused.

"His wealth is taken. His children are lost. His body is broken by illness. Friends come to comfort him, but soon they turn into judges, offering explanations disguised as wisdom. *You must have done something wrong,* they say. *There must be a reason.*"

Guruji's gaze moved slowly across the hall.

"But Job refuses easy answers. He does not deny God, yet he does not accept shallow consolation. He demands something deeper. He asks *why*. He asks for justice. He asks for logic behind his pain."

The hall grew still.

"And when God finally responds," Guruji continued, "He does not offer a justification. He does not explain suffering. He does not lay out a moral equation."

He let the silence stretch.

"Instead, God asks Job, 'Where were you when I laid the foundations of the earth? Tell me, if you have understanding.'"

The words seemed to widen the space around them.

"God speaks of the morning stars singing together, of oceans held by invisible boundaries, of creatures Job has never seen and forces he cannot command. Not to belittle Job—but to expand him."

Guruji's voice softened.

"This is not humiliation. It is an invitation into humility. Job is not being silenced; he is being reoriented. He is reminded that the universe is not small enough to fit inside human reasoning."

He leaned forward slightly.

"Job is not told to stop questioning. He is asked to remember the scale of what he is questioning—and the mystery within which his life unfolds."

Guruji paused once more.

"And in that remembering, something shifts. Job no longer needs an explanation. Presence replaces argument. Trust replaces demand."

He looked up gently.

"Sometimes," Guruji said, "the deepest answer to suffering is not *why*—but the recognition that we are standing inside a vastness that exceeds our understanding, yet does not exclude our pain."

A Whisper from Sufi Wisdom

Guruji's eyes softened further.

"A Sufi master once said, 'Sell your cleverness and buy bewilderment; cleverness is mere opinion, bewilderment is intuition.'"

He nodded gently.

"In Sufism, *hayra*—holy bewilderment—is not confusion. It is the state of standing before the Infinite without armor."

"To honour the unknowable," Guruji said, "is to let intelligence mature into humility."

He gestured toward the open windows.

"The sky does not demand to be understood before it offers light. The ocean does not require explanation before it carries ships. Life itself moves forward without waiting for our conclusions."

He looked at Alice.

"When we stop demanding final answers, curiosity becomes sacred. Silence becomes intelligent. Ethics arise naturally—because when you know you do not fully know, you act carefully, gently, responsibly."

Guruji ended with a quiet story.

"A child once asked her grandmother how deep the sky was. The grandmother replied, 'Deep enough that birds never hit its end.'"

He smiled.

"The child did not measure the sky. She trusted it."

Guruji's voice lowered to a whisper.

"The unknown is not a void to be conquered. It is a presence to be lived with—through wonder, restraint, and care."

The hall was still.

Not with answers—

but with reverence.

Sofia asked, "Guruji, **Can reason coexist with mystery?**

Guruji received Sofia's question with a quiet nod, as though it had already been echoing in the hall long before it was spoken.

He let a breath pass. Then another. When he spoke, his words moved slowly, like a river that knows both its banks and its depth.

Reason and Mystery

"Sofia," Guruji said, "reason and mystery are not enemies standing on opposite shores. They are two currents of the same river, flowing at different depths."

He looked toward the open windows, where light and shadow met without conflict.

"Reason clarifies what can be traced—patterns, causes, proportions, relationships. It gives structure to experience, much like grammar gives structure to language. Without reason, thought dissolves into chaos."

He paused.

"But mystery," he continued, "holds what cannot be reduced to structure. It is the silence beneath the sentence, the space that allows meaning to breathe."

"In the *Mundaka Upanishad*," Guruji said, "two birds sit on the same tree. One eats the fruit; the other watches."

He let the image settle.

"The bird that eats is reason—engaging, analysing, tasting the world. The bird that watches is mystery—silent, untouched, whole. Liberation comes not from killing one bird, but from recognising both."

A Parable from the Bible

Guruji continued, "In the Gospel of Luke, Mary hears that she will bear a child by divine mystery. She does not demand explanation, nor does she reject understanding. She asks one clear, rational question: 'How can this be?'"

He smiled gently.

"And then she says, 'Let it be unto me.' Reason asks; mystery receives. Neither denies the other."

A Sufi Teaching

"In Sufi tradition," Guruji said, "Rumi writes, 'Sell your cleverness and buy bewilderment.' He does not say destroy cleverness—he says sell it when it claims supremacy."

He raised his finger slightly.

"Cleverness that bows becomes wisdom. Bewilderment that listens becomes insight."

"When reason forgets mystery," Guruji said, "it hardens into certainty and begins to dominate. It demands closure where openness is needed. This is how ideologies are born."

"When mystery rejects reason," he continued, "it drifts into superstition, fear, and blind belief. This is how confusion masquerades as faith."

He looked directly at Sofia.

"Mature consciousness allows reason to explore without claiming final authority—and allows mystery to remain without fear."

Guruji said softly.

"A mathematician once tried to calculate the beauty of a sunset. He measured wavelengths, angles, refraction. A poet stood beside him and wept."

Guruji smiled.

"The mathematician was not wrong. The poet was not irrational. The tragedy would be if either believed the other unnecessary."

Silence followed.

Not the silence of ignorance—

but the silence where intelligence bows to wholeness.

Bhavya asked, "Guruji, Why do beliefs turn violent?"

Guruji listened to Bhavya's question with great tenderness. It was not a question born of curiosity alone, but of sorrow—sorrow at what humans have done to one another in the name of what they call truth.

He remained silent for a long moment. Then he spoke, slowly, as one who knows the weight of each word.

When Belief Hardens

"Bhavya," Guruji said, "beliefs turn violent when they stop being windows and become walls."

He looked around the hall, meeting no one's eyes and yet meeting everyone.

"A belief is meant to orient the mind, like a compass. It points. It does not imprison. But when a belief becomes identity—when a person says *I am this belief*—then any challenge to the belief feels like an attack on existence itself."

He paused.

"And fear enters."

The Blind Men and the Elephant

"You may know the old story," Guruji continued, "from Indian and Buddhist traditions—the blind men touching an elephant."

"One touches the leg and says, 'Truth is a pillar.' Another touches the trunk and says, 'Truth is a snake.' Another touches the ear and says, 'Truth is a fan.' Each is sincere. Each is partially correct. And yet they fight—ready to wound one another—over what the elephant *really* is."

He leaned forward slightly.

"The violence does not come from blindness. It comes from certainty."

"In the Bible," Guruji said, "Jesus is asked, 'What is truth?' He does not answer. Instead, he remains silent."

Guruji's voice softened.

"Because the moment truth is reduced to a sentence, someone will kill to defend it."

He added quietly, "Even the cross was built by people convinced they were right."

"In Sufism," Guruji continued, "there is a saying: 'The one who knows, knows he does not know.'"

He smiled faintly.

"Sufis dance not because they lack belief, but because belief has melted into love. Love does not need enemies."

The Root of Violence

"Violence," Guruji said, "does not arise from belief itself. It arises from insecurity."

"When a belief is fragile, it demands obedience. When it is rooted in insight, it invites dialogue."

He let the silence deepen.

"Spiritual conflict is born when partial perception demands total allegiance—when a fragment claims to be the whole."

The Way Back to Peace

"Peace returns," Guruji said, "when beliefs are held lightly—as maps, not territories."

"A map is useful," he said, "but no one bleeds to defend a map."

He looked at Bhavya with quiet compassion.

"When truth is allowed to remain larger than any single formulation, the heart relaxes. And a relaxed heart has no need to strike."

The hall remained still.

Some beliefs loosened their grip.

And in that loosening, something gentler became possible.

CHAPTER VI

How the One Becomes Many

"Death is not an erasure of existence, but a grammatical shift—being conjugated in another tense."

– Shree Shambav.

Synopsis

This chapter explores impermanence without descending into nihilism, revealing death not as negation but as transformation. Through silence, story, and metaphor, Guruji reframes birth and death as shifts of posture within a single, continuous substance. Just as clay remains when a pot breaks, existence endures even as forms dissolve. Drawing from ancient wisdom, natural observation, and quiet insight, the teaching dissolves fear by relocating meaning—from permanence of form to continuity of being. Individual identities are seen as temporary expressions, not ultimate realities. Grief is honoured, not dismissed, but freed from despair by a deeper understanding of change. Rebirth is approached both symbolically and cosmically, emphasising renewal without fixation. The chapter gently invites the reader to loosen attachment to names and roles, discovering peace not in what lasts forever, but in what never truly disappears.

After the evening break, the devotees returned to the Buddha Hall as though guided by an unseen rhythm—like leaves carried back to the river by a slow, faithful current. Outside, the world was changing robes. The sky darkened into a deep indigo, and the first stars emerged shyly, then with growing confidence, as if remembering an ancient duty. The moon rose without urgency, unconcerned with human clocks, following a path it had traced long before names were given to time.

Night found its voice in layers. Frogs sang near the water in patient cycles. Insects hummed like fine strings of an unseen veena. Somewhere, a bird called once, then again, passing sound from one shadow to another. A cool breeze wandered through the corridors, carrying the scent of damp earth and crushed leaves, brushing faces gently—as if reminding everyone that life does not sleep when humans fall silent.

Inside the Buddha Hall, lamps glowed with quiet resolve. Their flames did not flicker for attention; they simply were. Shadows settled into their places. The devotees took their seats—not merely with expectation, but with a subtle inward ripeness. The day's teachings had softened something. Defences had thinned. Listening had become less an effort and more a state.

After a few minutes, Guruji entered.

There was no announcement, no cue. And yet the hall knew. Conversations faded mid-breath. Bodies straightened as if guided from within. The restless movements of thought slowed. He walked to his asana with the unhurried ease of one who had never believed time to be scarce. When he sat, silence spread—not hollow, not oppressive, but alive, like a lake at dusk holding both sky and star in its stillness.

Guruji closed his eyes for a moment. Even the night outside seemed to lean in.

Then he spoke.

"A pot broke," Guruji said softly. "Clay remains."

The words fell into the hall like a stone into deep water—simple on the surface, endless beneath.

He continued, his voice calm, almost conversational:

"Birth and death are shifts of mode. Nothing truly dies—it changes posture."

The devotees listened, not rushing to understand, sensing that this was not a statement to be grasped but a space to be entered.

"Look around you," Guruji said. "What you call *things* are not fixed entities. They are gestures of one substance."

He gestured gently, as if encompassing the hall, the forest, the sky beyond.

"A tree, a river, a human body, a planet—each is a temporary expression, a particular posture adopted by existence for a time."

He paused.

"When we say a pot is born, we forget the clay. When we say the pot has died, we still forget the clay."

A few heads bowed instinctively.

"In the *Upanishads*," Guruji continued, "it is said: *'Just as gold is one, though it takes many forms, so is the Self one, though it appears as many.'*"

He smiled faintly.

"When a golden ring melts, do we mourn the death of gold? No. We only say the ring has changed its shape."

He then recalled the Buddha's own teaching.

"The Buddha spoke of *anicca*—impermanence—not to make us despair, but to free us from confusion. What changes was never meant to be held as permanent."

"In Taoism," Guruji said, "death is called 'returning.' Laozi writes: *'Returning is the movement of the Tao.'*"

"And in the Sufi tradition," he added, "they say the wave does not die when it falls back into the ocean—it remembers what it always was."

He looked gently at the devotees.

"Even modern science whispers the same truth. Matter is not destroyed; it transforms. Energy does not vanish; it shifts its dance."

"Birth and death," Guruji said, "are not beginnings and endings. They are changes of mode—like waking and sleeping, like standing and sitting."

He touched the floor lightly.

"This body is one posture of the infinite. When it can no longer hold that posture, existence stands up differently."

His voice softened.

"Nothing truly dies. It only changes posture."

The Quiet After

No one moved. No one needed to.

The night continued its song outside. The moon climbed a little higher. Somewhere, clay waited patiently to become pot, to become dust, to become something unnamed.

And in the Buddha Hall, something loosened—fear perhaps, or grief, or the tight knot around the idea of ending.

The pot had broken.

The clay remained.

Martina's question rose gently, yet it carried the weight of many unspoken nights.

"Guruji," she asked, her voice barely stirring the stillness, "how does this view change grief?"

Guruji did not answer immediately. His eyes rested on the lamp before him, its flame steady yet forever changing. Then he spoke, slowly, as one speaks to a wound that must not be startled.

"When death is seen as annihilation," he said, "grief becomes a cliff. The heart stands at its edge, staring into nothingness, terrified that love has been swallowed by a void. But when death is understood as transformation, grief does not disappear—it learns to walk. It bends. It changes posture."

He paused, allowing the words to settle.

"Loss still hurts," Guruji continued. "Understanding does not anaesthetise love. If anything, it proves love was real. But despair softens, because what you loved has not vanished—it has changed its way of being present."

Guruji said, "A grieving son once approached the sage Yajnavalkya. His father had died, and the boy's sorrow was raw, unanswered. With trembling urgency, he asked, '*Where has my father gone?*'"

Guruji paused, allowing the weight of the question to settle.

"Yajnavalkya did not respond with theology or consolation. He did not speak of heavens or rebirth. Instead, he asked for a bowl of water."

The hall leaned inward.

"The sage took a small handful of salt and dropped it into the water. He stirred gently until the crystals disappeared. Then he turned to the boy and asked, '*Where is the salt now?*'"

A quiet understanding passed through the listeners.

"'It is everywhere,' the boy replied. 'I cannot see it, but I can taste it in every drop.'"

Guruji nodded softly.

"'Exactly,' Yajnavalkya said. 'What was visible has not been destroyed—it has become pervasive.'"

Guruji looked around the hall.

"The father the boy loved was once a form—recognizable, tangible, familiar. But that form was never the whole truth. What has dissolved has not vanished; it has simply moved beyond the reach of the eyes."

He spoke gently now.

"In grief, we search desperately for the form we loved—the voice, the face, the presence we could touch. And in doing so, we overlook the presence that remains—subtle, spread everywhere, no longer confined to a single body."

He paused.

"Love does not disappear when form dissolves. It changes its mode. Like salt in water, it can no longer be pointed to—but it can be felt in everything."

Guruji lowered his voice.

"Grief is not only the pain of loss. It is the struggle of perception—learning to sense what can no longer be seen."

The silence that followed was not empty. It was full.

After a long pause, Guruji spoke of the Buddha.

"There is a story of the Buddha standing in silence as Kisagotami wept before him, her dead child clutched in her arms. She had gone from house to house begging for medicine, convinced that somewhere there must be a cure for death."

The hall felt hushed.

"The Buddha did not interrupt her grief. He did not tell her that death was inevitable, nor did he offer philosophy to quiet her pain. He looked at her with compassion and gave her a simple task."

Guruji's voice remained soft.

"He asked her to bring him a handful of mustard seeds—but only from a house that had never known death."

A faint stillness spread through the room.

"Kisagotami went from door to door. Every home had mustard seeds. And every home had also known loss—a parent, a child, a spouse, a loved one taken by death. By the time she returned, her hands were empty, but her heart had changed."

Guruji looked up.

"The Buddha had not denied her pain. He had widened her understanding. Without argument or explanation, he led her to see that her suffering was not unique, not singled out by fate, but woven into the shared condition of human life."

He paused.

"In that realization, something softened. Grief loosened its grip—not because the child was forgotten, but because Kisagotami was no longer alone in her sorrow."

Guruji concluded quietly,

"Grief begins to heal when it realizes it is shared. Compassion arises when suffering is seen as universal. And wisdom dawns when pain is met not with resistance, but with understanding."

He drew from the Psalms as well: *'Though I walk through the valley of the shadow of death, I fear no evil.'*

"Notice," he said, "it is a valley, not an abyss. One walks through."

Grief, he explained, becomes less about clinging to absence and more about learning new forms of relationship—through memory that shapes character, influence that continues in others, matter that returns to earth, and meaning that ripples forward in time. Like a river that disappears underground only to re-emerge miles later, love does not stop flowing when it vanishes from sight.

"This view does not rush mourning," Guruji said softly. "It dignifies it. Tears are still sacred. Longing is still human. But grief no longer demands collapse."

He looked at Martina, his gaze kind and steady.

"You learn," he said, "to carry sorrow without drowning in it, to remember without denying change, and to love without trying to imprison what must move on. Grief remains—but it matures. It becomes a quiet devotion to continuity, rather than a protest against reality."

Beatrice's question lingered in the hall like a bell whose echo had not yet found its rest.

"Guruji," she asked, "is rebirth literal or symbolic?"

Guruji smiled—not with certainty, but with spaciousness. He looked at the night sky visible through the high window, where the moon had shifted slightly since his last words, unchanged yet never the same.

"Rebirth," he said gently, "need not be imprisoned inside a single meaning. Truth often breathes through more than one doorway."

He leaned forward slightly, as if inviting the question closer rather than pushing an answer outward.

"On the literal level," Guruji continued, "nothing ends. Substance rearranges. The body returns to elements; breath to air; warmth to fire. Atoms that once formed a hand may become leaf, river, or star-dust. Karma, too, is continuity—causes seeking their effects, like seeds carried by wind until they find soil." He paused. "In this sense, rebirth is movement, not migration."

He recalled an ancient image from the *Bhagavad Gita*: *'As a person discards worn-out garments and puts on new ones, so the embodied self discards old bodies and enters others.'* "But notice," Guruji said, "the teaching points not to a traveller clinging to form, but to life's refusal to stop."

Then he shifted the lens.

"Symbolically," he said, "rebirth happens far more often than we admit. Every time an identity collapses—'I am this role, this wound, this belief'—and something truer takes its place, a rebirth has occurred. When arrogance dies into humility, when fear dissolves into trust, when ignorance opens into understanding—something has died, and something has been born."

He told a Sufi story of a disciple who came to his master saying, "I am lost." The master replied, "Good. The one who thought he knew the way has died." "That," Guruji said, "is rebirth."

Even the Bible whispers this truth, he reminded them: *'Unless a grain of wheat falls into the earth and dies, it remains alone; but if it dies, it bears much fruit.'*

"Here," Guruji said, "death is not punishment—it is participation in renewal."

He looked back at Beatrice.

"When rebirth is taken only literally, the mind argues. When taken only symbolically, the cosmos feels reduced. Wisdom allows both without forcing agreement."

He let the silence deepen.

"Rebirth," Guruji said, "is continuity without fixation. Life renewing itself without repeating its masks. Whether across lifetimes or within a single breath, the teaching is the same: do not cling to what you are. What you are becoming is already on its way."

The lamps flickered softly, as if nodding.

Emma's question arose quietly, yet it carried the weight of something many had felt but few had dared to ask.

"Guruji," she said, her voice steady but inwardly trembling, "what remains after identity dissolves?"

Guruji did not answer at once. He looked around the Buddha Hall—the lamps, the faces, the shadows breathing along the walls. Then he said softly, "To ask this question is already to be standing at the edge of an old self."

"When names fall away," he began, "and roles loosen their grip—parent, seeker, success, failure—what disappears is not *you*, but the story you have been rehearsing to remember yourself." His voice was calm, almost tender. "What remains is not emptiness in the sense of absence. It is emptiness in the sense the sky is empty—vast, unburdened, capable of holding everything."

He offered an image from the *Upanishads*: a lump of salt dissolved in water. "You cannot point and say, 'Here is the salt,' yet taste the water anywhere, and it is present. Identity is the crystal. Awareness is the water. When the crystal dissolves, the essence does not vanish—it becomes everywhere."

Guruji then recalled an incident from the life of the Buddha.

"Once," he said, "the Buddha was asked what remains after enlightenment. The question came from an earnest place, but it carried an unexamined assumption—that awakening leaves behind something that can be pointed to, possessed, or described."

He paused.

"The Buddha did not answer. He remained silent."

The silence itself seemed deliberate.

"His silence was not refusal," Guruji explained. "It was instruction. The question assumes that enlightenment produces an object—some lasting state, identity, or attainment. But awakening dissolves the very structure that turns experience into an object."

Guruji leaned forward slightly.

"What remains is not *something*. What remains is the subject before it became an object to itself—the seeing before it was named, the awareness before it began describing itself as 'me.'"

He let the words settle.

"After awakening, there is no enlightened self left standing to admire enlightenment. There is only clear presence, functioning without a centre."

After a moment, Guruji continued.

"This understanding is not limited to Buddhism."

He then quoted from Christian mysticism, his voice steady:

"Meister Eckhart once said, '*The eye with which I see God is the same eye with which God sees me.*'"

Guruji looked around the hall.

"This is not poetry for effect," he said. "It is a precise pointing. Eckhart is describing awareness without biography—seeing without a personal centre, knowing without a separate knower."

He paused.

"When the eye that sees is no longer claimed as *mine*, the division between seeker and sought collapses. There is no observer standing apart from the sacred."

Guruji said softly,

"When Yajnavalkya says *neti, neti*, when the Buddha remains silent, and when Eckhart speaks of a single eye, they are all protecting the same truth—from being reduced to an idea, an experience, or a possession."

"The highest understanding," Guruji said, "kneels before mystery—not because it is confused, but because it knows the limits of words."

He turned to a simple story.

A man once asked the ocean, "What happens to the wave when it dies?"

The ocean replied, "It never was separate enough to die."

"Identity," Guruji continued, "is a posture life takes for a time. When that posture relaxes, life does not end—it rests in itself."

He looked gently at Emma.

"What remains," he said, "is presence without boundary, love without ownership, knowing without a knower. Nothing personal survives—but nothing essential is lost. Only the illusion of separation dissolves. And in that dissolution, you do not disappear."

He paused, letting the words settle like dust into stillness.

"You finally arrive," he said, "where you have always been."

After a long pause, Guruji rose quietly from his asana. Without announcement or final words, he left the Buddha Hall, bringing the day's teachings—and the retreat itself—to a gentle close. The devotees followed in silence, each carrying something inward that words could not yet hold.

The Buddha Hall soon emptied of its human presence, yet its essence remained—warm, luminous, and subtly charged, as though the silence itself still remembered Guruji. Above, the sky stretched wide and clear. Stars shimmered as passing clouds played hide-and-seek with their light. A soft wind moved through the courtyards, stirring leaves into quiet conversation. Frogs sang their nocturnal hymns near unseen waters, insects hummed in steady rhythm, and night birds called from shadowed branches. Even in stillness, life spoke—reminding those who listened that the night, too, was a teacher.

Gradually, the devotees made their way to the Annapoorneshwara food centre for the evening meal.

After dinner, Vidyarthi, Aastha, Akshaya, Kiran, Padma, Vasudeva, and Abhirami gathered near a small fireplace. Flames danced against the cool night air, casting moving shadows across their faces. Warmth spread easily—through fire, shared presence, and the quiet intimacy of friendship. Their conversation flowed without effort: personal reflections intertwined with the day's teachings, gentle laughter mingling with thoughtful silence.

Soon others joined them. Bhavya, Aarna, Dev, Kiran, Sam, Alice, Sofia, and John arrived, their voices blending with the soft crackle of burning wood. Nita, Lalitha, Rohith, and Sujitha followed, adding new threads to the shared tapestry of conversation.

Moments later, Akshatha, Apeksha, Abhilasha, Akanksh, and Roopa appeared, their faces still illuminated by the day's contemplations. Behind them came Kieron, Astyn, Espen, Greta, and Divyani, carrying with them the quiet excitement of anticipation. Soon Aurora, Ginevra, Emma, Giorgia, Greta, Martina, and Beatrice joined the circle, completing the gathering.

Then Abhilasha's voice rose gently above the murmurs, calm yet expectant.

"Time for Apeksha's story…"

Apeksha did not begin at once. She looked into the fire, watching a log collapse inward as its outer form surrendered to glow. When she spoke, her voice was low, steady, as though she were not inventing the story but remembering it.

"Guruji once told me this," she said.

There was once a lamp-maker who lived on the edge of a village, where the forest thinned and the stars felt close enough to overhear human thoughts.

He shaped lamps from clay—simple, unadorned vessels. People came to him not for beauty, but for reliability. His lamps did not flicker in wind; they did not crack in heat.

One evening, a traveller arrived carrying a broken lamp. Its body was intact, but the flame would not hold.

'Fix it,' the traveller said. 'This lamp has guided me through many nights.'

The lamp-maker examined it and then did something unexpected. He broke the lamp completely.

The traveller cried out, 'You've destroyed it!'

The lamp-maker gathered the shards gently and said, 'No. I have released the clay from a shape it no longer needs.'

He placed the fragments into water, kneaded them back into softness, and reshaped the clay—not into a lamp this time, but into a small bowl.

When it dried, he placed water inside and held it beneath the moon.

'This,' he said, 'will now reflect light instead of holding it.'

The traveller watched the moon tremble on the water's surface and understood.

Apeksha paused. The fire cracked softly, as if affirming the silence.

"We think usefulness lies in staying the same," she continued. "But life asks us to change roles without believing we have ceased to exist. What ends is not essence—only function."

She glanced around the circle. Faces were still, receptive.

"Today, Guruji spoke of postures," she said. "Birth, death, identity, grief—all postures of the same substance. The tragedy is not that the lamp breaks, but that we refuse to become the bowl."

No one spoke. The night seemed to lean closer.

"One day," Apeksha said, "even the bowl will return to clay. And the clay—to earth. And the earth—to stars. Nothing is wasted. Nothing is lost. Only the story changes its shape."

The fire burned lower. One by one, the devotees rose—not abruptly, but as leaves loosen from a branch when the time is right. Goodnights were exchanged softly, like blessings.

As they walked back toward their chambers, the teachings of the day did not feel heavy or demanding. They felt companionable—walking beside them in the dark.

Behind them, the embers glowed on, holding the memory of flame.

And above Kanchipuram, the stars remained—silent witnesses to forms dissolving, postures shifting, and the endless continuity that needs no name.

EPILOGUE

After the Last Vibration

"Nothing in existence is ever lost—only reconfigured into a form your memory has not yet learned to love."

– Shree Shambav.

Every journey ends not with an answer, but with listening.

This book began in silence—before form, before explanation—and it ends in the same place. Not because nothing has been said, but because what truly matters can no longer be spoken. Words have traced the contours of unity, but unity itself remains untouched by language. What has been offered here is not a doctrine to believe, nor a system to defend, but a way of seeing—a remembering.

Through Shree Shambav's vision, the reader has been invited to look beyond appearances without rejecting them, to move through form without forgetting substance. God has not been placed above the world, nor hidden behind ritual, nor reduced to concept. God has been revealed as frequency—the living coherence beneath breath, matter, emotion, thought, birth, and death. Not an object of worship, but the very condition of existence.

You have seen how the One does not become many by breaking, but by expressing. How nature is not separate from spirit, but its visible body. How suffering is not a flaw in creation, but a distortion of perception. How death is not an ending, but a change of posture within an unbroken continuity. How knowledge must bow before mystery, and how humility is not weakness but intelligence in its most refined form.

And yet—this is not the end.

Because understanding unity is not the same as living it.

This first volume has turned the gaze inward and outward at once, restoring wholeness to what was divided. But a deeper question now quietly arises:

If reality is one, how then shall we live?

How does unity move through choice, action, pain, responsibility, love, and time?

How does the God Frequency express itself through karma, ethics, reason, and the human journey? How does the soul return—not as escape, but as participation?

These questions do not belong to theory. They belong to life.

Volume Two of *The God Frequency* will continue this unfolding—not by leaving Singularity behind, but by allowing it to walk, suffer, decide, and love through the human story. It will explore the soul's journey within a deterministic cosmos, karma not as punishment but as experience, and pain as a teacher rather than an enemy. It will examine ethics not as imposed morality, but as natural alignment with the One. It will reveal reason as devotion, and love of God not as emotion, but as clear understanding lived without division.

This is not a sequel—it is a deepening.

Until then, the teaching does not wait in pages.

It breathes as you.

It listens as you.

It moves through your choices, your silences, your courage to remain open.

The God Frequency has never stopped sounding.

May you learn to hear it—not as something new, but as what has always been quietly singing you into being.

—*End of Volume One*

Life Coach and Philanthropist

Shree Shambav is the visionary founder of the Shree Shambav Ayur Rakshita Foundation (www.shambav-ayurrakshita.org). He founded this institution with a lofty goal: to recognise human identity across gender, ethnicity, and nationality. Through this organisation, he wants to assist all communities in realising their full potential and the intrinsic beauty of life.

Shree Shambav, a Life Coach, is dedicated to supporting people on their journeys of self-discovery and empowerment. He assists people in discovering who they are, determining what inspires and drives them, and overcoming limiting ideas. His approach clarifies what one wants in life, assisting people through goal-setting and a step-by-step process for achieving them. He empowers people to make deliberate and responsible decisions, allowing them to identify their blind spots and evolve as individuals via the use of numerous strategies and tools.

The foundation's bold, uncompromising, and compassionate ventures are always aimed at initiating the "Inner Transformation" process. They focus on spiritual growth, personal growth, and self-healing while emphasising that true progress lies in "Inclusive Growth and Co-existence." This philosophy drives all their initiatives, encouraging a holistic approach to development and well-being.

Under Shree Shambav's leadership, the foundation has launched several impactful movements:

Shree Shambav Green Movement: This mission is to create a healthy, green, and clean earth through responsible water conservation and greening initiatives. The movement strives to make the world a green paradise by encouraging sustainable living and environmental responsibility.

Shree Shambav Vidya Vedhika (Vizhuthugal): This project aims to help students and children by offering training, books, stationery, and uniforms. It aims to provide the next generation with the tools and resources they need to excel both academically and personally.

Shree Shambav and his foundation exemplify the spirit of compassion, transformation, and inclusive growth via their work, which has a profound impact on individuals and communities around the world. His work exemplifies the power of acknowledging and nourishing the human spirit, creating a world in which everyone can reach their full potential and appreciate the beauty of life.

TESTIMONIALS

Journey of Soul - Karma - "We die in our twenties and are buried at eighty." Remember that nothing can stop someone who refuses to be stopped. "Most people do not fail; they simply give up." Shree Shambav deserves full credit. It allowed me to sit and consider what I might miss out on in life. The author has delved into every aspect of our daily lives. How can a seemingly insignificant change in these seemingly insignificant details bring us such joy? The Soul of Journey teaches you the "art of living" as well as the "art of dying."

Twenty + One Series - The rich cultural heritage offered a host in twenty + one short stories with incredible imagination, morals and values prevalent at a given time, influencing how people respond to a crisis or any situation. The author has recreated images with universal values and morals. The plentiful of fascinating from faraway lands would leave the modern play and story writers a cringe. The book supports trust and immeasurable values instilling hope for the new generations.

Death - "Shree Shambav's 'Death - Light of Life and the Shadow of Death' is an extraordinary masterpiece that delves deep into the profound questions surrounding our existence and mortality. The book's opening statement, 'Nothing ever truly dies; it simply ceases to exist in one form before resuming it in another,' sets the stage for a thought-provoking exploration of death's multifaceted nature. Shambav's remarkable ability to navigate the philosophical complexities of death and our universal fear of it is both enlightening and comforting. This book is a testament to the power of understanding and acceptance."

Whispers of Eternity - "Reading 'Whispers of Eternity' by Shree Shambav was a transformative experience that left me captivated from beginning to end. Each section of this exquisite collection delves into the myriad facets of existence, offering poignant reflections on life, death, and everything in between. Shree Shambav's verses are a testament to the beauty of language and the power of expression, inviting readers to embark on a journey of self-discovery and spiritual awakening. Whether celebrating life's simple joys or grappling with the complexities of human emotion, this book is a timeless companion that speaks to the heart and soul of every reader."

Life Changing Journey Series - "Life Changing Journey Series II Inspirational Quotes" is a remarkable collection that illuminates the path to self-discovery and personal growth. With its inspiring quotes and insightful reflections, this book serves as a beacon of light in a world often shrouded in darkness. Each quote offers wisdom, guidance, and encouragement, reminding readers of their inner strength and resilience. A must-read for anyone seeking inspiration and enlightenment.

Learn To Love Yourself – "A Heartfelt Guide to Authentic Self-Love." "Learn to Love Yourself" invites readers on a transformative journey to embrace their true essence in a world often focused on external validation. Through ten insightful chapters, it gently reveals principles of genuine self-love, guiding readers to deepen their connection with themselves. Beyond surface positivity, it encourages the cultivation of resilient self-acceptance, from embracing one's unique qualities to setting empowering boundaries. With inspiring stories and practical wisdom, this book is a trusted companion on the path to inner peace, fulfilment, and joy, helping readers build lives that reflect their authentic selves.

The Power of Letting Go – This book has been a gift to my spiritual journey. Shree Shambav's insights into attachment, personal growth cycles, and forgiveness are enlightening. The concept of seven-year cycles resonated with me, helping me understand the natural phases of life. I feel more empowered to let go of what no longer serves me and step into a life of freedom and fulfilment. A truly beautiful read!

A Journey of Lasting Peace – "A Journey of Lasting Peace" feels like a trusted friend guiding you through the maze of self-discovery. The 18 transformative principles are both practical and deeply resonant, addressing everything from gratitude practices to the art of letting go. Each chapter is infused with warmth and wisdom, making it easy to apply the concepts to my life. I particularly appreciated the emphasis on physical health's connection to mental well-being; it served as a wake-up call for me to prioritise my health. This book is an invaluable resource for anyone serious about personal growth!

Astrology Unveiled Series – "Profound, Logical, and Inspiring". What stands out in Astrology Unveiled is the author's dedication to making Vedic astrology logical and approachable. Each concept flows naturally into the next, backed by examples and exercises. The insights into karma and life cycles add a philosophical depth rarely seen in astrology books. Perfect for anyone seeking spiritual growth alongside astrological knowledge!

The Entitlement Trap - "Thought-Provoking and Challenging" The book challenges readers to confront their own sense of entitlement, and that's not easy—but it's essential. The Entitlement Trap doesn't offer a one-size-fits-all approach. Instead, it's a thoughtful, layered examination of how entitlement can limit our growth. The chapter on "Defining Your Own Hill" was particularly impactful, as it pushed me to reconsider which challenges are truly worth pursuing. A thought-provoking read for those willing to do the inner work to create a life they can be proud of.

Whispers of a Dying Soul – "A Soul-Stirring Reflection on Life's Unspoken Truths" **-** *Whispers of a Dying Soul: Unspoken Regrets and Unlived Dreams"* is a deeply moving exploration of the unexpressed emotions and unfulfilled aspirations that shape our lives in ways we often don't realise. This book invites readers to confront the powerful, often hidden impact of regret while guiding them through a journey of introspection and healing. Each page opens a space to reflect on the choices that define us—from moments of unspoken love to neglected passions—offering a gentle reminder to live authentically and courageously.

Whispers of the Soul: A Journey Through Haiku - is a mesmerising collection that speaks directly to the heart. Each haiku is a delicate brushstroke capturing life's fleeting beauty and timeless wisdom, inviting readers into moments of deep reflection and peace. This book is a balm for the soul, guiding us to find meaning in stillness and connection in simplicity. The themes of nature, love, and mindfulness echo universal truths, resonating with quiet, powerful grace. It's a book to be savoured slowly, cherished deeply, and returned to often. Truly, a gift for anyone seeking calm and clarity in life's chaos.

Whispers of Silence - Unlocking Inner Power through Stillness by Shree Shambav is a rare gem that beckons readers to pause, reflect, and reconnect with their inner selves. In a world that never stops talking, this book offers a profound exploration of silence—not as a void but as a rich and transformative space.

From the first page, Shree Shambav's writing resonates deeply, blending scientific insights with spiritual wisdom in a way that feels both universal and deeply personal. The author's ability to bridge the tangible and the transcendent makes this book an invaluable guide for anyone navigating the chaos of modern life.

The Power of Words: Transforming Speech, Transforming Lives - "The Power of Words is a profound and enlightening guide that has transformed the way I approach communication. Shree Shambav masterfully uncovers the hidden influence of our words on relationships, self-perception, and overall well-being. This book doesn't just teach you how to speak; it inspires mindful communication that fosters connection and trust. The insights on replacing negative patterns like gossip and judgment with kindness and authenticity are truly life-changing. The practical strategies and engaging narratives make it an invaluable resource for personal and professional growth. A must-read for anyone striving to communicate with intention, clarity, and compassion. Highly recommended!"

The Art of Intentional Living: Minimalism for a Life of Purpose - "The Art of Intentional Living is a refreshing guide to finding clarity in a cluttered world. With practical wisdom and profound insights, it inspires you to simplify, prioritise, and live with purpose. A must-read for anyone seeking balance and fulfilment."

Awakening the Infinite: The Power of Consciousness in Transforming Life - "Awakening the Infinite is a transformative guide that expands the mind and nourishes the soul. With profound insights and practical wisdom, this book beautifully explores the power of consciousness, helping readers connect with their true purpose and inner potential. It is a journey of self-discovery, healing, and spiritual awakening, offering clarity and inspiration at every turn. A must-read for anyone looking to live with greater awareness, meaning, and authenticity."

Beyond the Veil: A Journey Through Life After Death:

"This book touched me in ways few others have—it's not just about death, but about life, meaning, and the vast unknown that connects them. Beyond the Veil offers a graceful blend of science and spirit, inviting us to explore the mystery with awe rather than fear. The stories, insights, and reflections linger in your heart long after the final page. A truly transformative read that brings light on the shadows of mortality. It reminded me that in embracing death, we truly learn how to live."

Bonds Beyond Blood:

"A profoundly moving story that reminds us, family is not defined by blood, but by love, sacrifice, and the courage to heal. Every chapter touched my soul with its emotional truth and timeless wisdom. Through joy, grief, and redemption, this book captures the raw beauty of human connection. I saw reflections of my own family in its pages—both the pain and the hope. A powerful, unforgettable read that lingers long after the final word."

A Journey into Spiritual Maturity: 12 Golden Rules for Inner Transformation

"This book is a gentle yet powerful guide that awakened a deeper sense of purpose within me. Each golden rule felt like a mirror reflecting truths I needed to embrace. Shree Shambav's wisdom is timeless, poetic, and profoundly grounding. It's not just a read—it's a journey into the heart of who you truly are. A must-read for anyone seeking lasting peace, clarity, and inner transformation."

The Inner Battlefield: Overcoming the Enemies of the Mind and Soul:

"This book is a powerful revelation—an honest mirror to the battles we fight within. Every chapter is a step closer to clarity, peace, and emotional mastery. Shree Shambav brilliantly transforms ancient wisdom into practical guidance for modern souls. It awakened in me a new strength to face my fears and rise above inner turmoil. A must-read for anyone seeking true inner victory and lasting transformation."

The Seeker's Gold – Unlocking Life's Greatest Treasure

The Seeker's Gold is a soul-stirring masterpiece that goes far beyond the pursuit of wealth—it is a journey into the heart of what truly matters. Each chapter unfolds with poetic wisdom and emotional depth, revealing that life's real treasure is not found in riches but in the transformation of the self. As the protagonist evolves through trials, love, and profound realisations, so does the reader. This book is a mirror for every dreamer, a lantern for every seeker, and a companion for anyone walking the path of purpose. A timeless tale that stays with you long after the final page.

Born to Rise Series I & II:

Born to Rise – Series I & II is a profound awakening—a journey that begins in silence and leads you to the core of your true power.

Series I reshapes your understanding of success, showing that clarity is more valuable than applause, and authenticity more powerful than performance.

Series II takes you deeper, unlocking the mindset and inner strategy behind meaningful, lasting growth—not just in wealth, but in wisdom.

Together, these books are not just guides—they are soul mirrors, revealing the truths you've forgotten and the strength you've always held.

This is more than reading—it's remembering who you are, and rising with purpose, not pressure.

The Law of Attraction: A Soulful Path

The Law of Attraction: A Soulful Path is more than a guide—it's a spiritual companion. Shree Shambav has beautifully woven timeless wisdom with practical tools, helping me understand that manifestation isn't about control—it's about inner alignment and grace. Each rule in this book felt like a key unlocking something dormant within me. I've read many books on the Law of Attraction, but none touched my heart like this one. Through soulful rituals, deep reflection, and gentle encouragement, I began releasing old fears and stepping into clarity and peace. This book helped me move from desperation to trust, from wanting to becoming. It's a must-read for anyone yearning for meaning, healing, and true, lasting transformation.

Whispers of Stillness: Where the soul listens beyond the noise Series

Whispers of Stillness is a rare and luminous work that speaks softly yet transforms deeply. Each couplet feels like a breath of wisdom—gentle, precise, and profoundly awakening. Moving gracefully through Virtue, Wealth, and Love, the series invites quiet reflection, ethical clarity, and emotional truth. This is not poetry to rush through, but to live with. A timeless companion for seekers, leaders, and sensitive hearts, it restores stillness where the soul can truly listen.

ACKNOWLEDGEMENTS

To my grandfathers, grandmothers, mothers, fathers, aunts, uncles, neighbours, sisters, brothers, friends, and teachers, they poured in endless moral stories, retellings of Ramayana, Mahabharata, Puranas, Upanishads, and so on.

My teachers, neighbours, and kindred souls. Who provided us with a stage to perform wonderful Puranic stories and were gracious enough to acknowledge our efforts.

The artists and translators of epics have served as a source of inspiration, invigorating our spirits, making these works accessible, and enabling us to grasp the profound depths and deeper dimensions they contain.

I also cherish the stimulating conversations; I had with my wonderful mothers, Punitha Muniswamy and Uma Devi.

Our family's youngest member, Aadhya, who always overwhelmed me with questions, inspired this book.

I would likewise prefer to express gratitude to Mr Sivakumar, Mrs Roopa Sivakumar, Mr Akshaya

Rajesh, Ms Akshatha Rajesh, Ms Apeksha Prabhu, Mr Akanksh Prabhu, Mr Nikash Sarasambi, and Mrs Spoorthi Nikash for their valuable inputs.

I must thank Mr Rajesh, Mr Savan Prabhu, Mrs Revathi Rajesh, Mrs Rajani Sarasambi, and Mrs Manju Reshma, who encouraged me and often suggested writing a book. Their unwavering belief that I had something valuable to offer kept me going during my writing sessions.

Love you all,

Shree Shambav

Web: www.shambav.org

Email: shreeshambav@gmail.com

9 789358 126310

Printed at Repro India Ltd.